Y0-DJO-668

Private Dreams, Shared Visions: Student Affairs Work in Small College

Edited by

George D. Kuh
Associate Dean for Academic Affairs
School of Education
Indiana University

Andrea C. McAleenan
Director, National Center for Partnership Development and
Training, Cities In Schools

Volume 5; NASPA Monograph Series
Published by the National Association
of Student Personnel Administrators, Inc.

Library of Congress Cataloging-in-Publication Data
Private dreams, shared visions.
    (NASPA Monograph series ; v. 5)
    Bibliography: p.
    1. Personnel service in higher education — United States. 2. Small colleges — United States. 3. College environment — United States. 4 College student personnel administrators — United States. I. Kuh, George D., 1946- . II. Title: Student affairs work in small colleges. III. McAleenan, Andrea C., 1944- . IV. Series.
LB2343.P73 1986   378'.194'0973   86-8379
ISBN 0-931654-07-6

NASPA Monograph Board 1985-86

Contents

Contributors

David P. Dodson is Dean of Students at the University of Puget Sound (WA).

Deborah L. Floyd, formerly Dean at Scott Community College (IA), is Vice President for Student Personnel at Collin County Community College District in Texas.

Rob Goffigon is the Coordinator of Placement at Seattle Pacific University (WA).

Kent T. Hawley, formerly Vice President for Student Affairs, is Director of International Programs at Wartburg College (IA).

Wanda Hendricks, formerly at McKendree College (IL), is the Director of Housing at North Carolina A&T State University.

George D. Kuh is Professor and Associate Dean for Academic Affairs in the School of Education at Indiana University.

Debra Lacey is Associate Dean of Students at George Fox College (OR).

Steve Larson is Associate Dean of Students at Gordon College (MA).

Cheryl Mabey is Dean for Student Development at Mount St. Mary's College (CA).

Andrea C. McAleenan, formerly Dean of Students at Gordon College (MA), is Director of the National Center for Partnership Education, Development Training, Cities in Schools, at Los Angeles (CA).

Rebecca Mattson, formerly Director of Career Planning and Placement, Whitman College (WA), is a Counselor in the Career Development Center at California State University-Fullerton.

Samuel Mazman is Dean of Student Personnel Services at West Shore Community College (MI).

Roger Morris, formerly Director of Student Programs at Gordon College (MA), is Director of Orientation at the University of Oregon.

Raymond P. Rood is the Chairman of the Department of Human Resources Development at Azusa Pacific University (CA).

Daryl G. Smith is Vice President for Planning and Research and Associate Professor of Psychology at Scripps College (CA).

Patricia M. Volp, formerly the Vice President and Dean of Students at St. Teresa College (MN), is Associate Dean of Students at Southeast Missouri State University.

Janet R. Wright is Assistant Dean for Student Development at Manchester College (IN).

Robert B. Young is Associate Professor of Higher Education Administration at Kent State University (OH).

Foreword

The contributors to this monograph share four beliefs. First, although the small college experience is not often addressed in our literature and/or at professional meetings, we believe that small colleges play an important, distinctive role in American higher education. For the purposes of this monograph, "small" is defined as a two year or four year institution of higher education with less than 5,000 students. We realize that a numerical definition of the small college is quite superficial and possibly misleading. In many instances, "small" is a frame of mind, a commitment to a pervasive influence of shared understandings and beliefs. Shared understandings lead to a salient, coherent institutional mission, a clarity of institutional purpose that has differentiated the role of the small college in a mass system of higher education. Student affairs work may lack purpose and meaning unless we are clear about what we believe, what we value, and what we are trying to accomplish within the context of the institutional mission.

Second, we believe that student affairs staff make important contributions to high quality living and learning experiences in small colleges. We are not so naive or chauvinistic to believe that student affairs staff are *the* critical ingredient in a developmentally powerful setting; nor that the small college is the only type of institution that encourages optimal levels of development. The pervasive influence of peers is well documented, and there are usually relatively few student affairs staff on small college campuses. But when we are familiar with what constitutes a developmentally powerful living and learning environment, and use this information to enhance the quality of students' experiences, we can make unique contributions, some of which are enumerated in the chapters that follow.

Third, we believe that student affairs work—in all kinds of institutions—is rooted in a noble cause: to recognize potential and promise in individual students and to maintain environments that encourage students to realize their potential. Most college students must contend with a myriad of interpersonal, intellectual, spiritual, and ethical challenges. To help students deal constructively with these challenges requires active listening, reflection, vision, and purposeful action on the part of student affairs staff. The Student Personnel Point of View provides a philosophical touchstone for our work, and few proponents of general education would quarrel with its tenets. But the diminished influence of general education has made it difficult to convince students that an important outcome of college is self-discovery and developing one's potential. Recognizing and encouraging the development of potential in students is not the exclusive province of student affairs staff, but it is an important part of our work.

Finally, we believe a liberating education requires interaction and collaboration among faculty, administration, staff, and students. The strength of the small college experience comes from the sense of community fostered when all members of the college work together and learn from one another. The limiting bonds of the past are released when new ideas inform feelings and habits, when valued traditions communicated by faculty are reinterpreted by students blazing their own trails, and when private dreams become shared visions.

The purpose of this monograph is to underscore the value of student affairs work to the small college mission. Much of what follows is not likely to surprise long-time observers of the small college scene. The monograph should be particularly useful to student affairs staff new to small colleges and to graduate students deciding what kind of institution will provide the best match between altruistic, service-oriented aspirations and personal development needs. Staff with considerable experience will hopefully find that the contributions touch some responsive chords, and that one or more of the chapters will stimulate reexamination of the student affairs mission on their own campus.

The idea for a NASPA-sponsored monograph about student affairs work in small colleges percolated for several years. Work on this publication began in earnest in the spring of 1984 following the Association's meeting in Louisville, Kentucky. We salute NASPA's commitment to examining the role of student affairs in small colleges, and we particularly appreciate the persistence of the contributors without whose patience, ideals, and ideas this project could not have been completed. Many others with rich insights into small college student affairs work could have easily been invited to contribute their ideas. We hope these chapters capture the sentiments they would like expressed.

Martha McGinty Stodt, Chairperson of the NASPA Monograph Board, deserves special recognition for the encouragement and support she provided throughout the project. We gratefully acknowledge the helpful comments and suggestions to improve the manuscript offered by Fred Preston and Gail Martin representing the NASPA Monograph Board, and the advice and expertise shared by Susan Bowling Komives, Dick Palm, Charles Schroeder, and Glenn Nicholls who reacted to various chapters. We are indebted to Ms. Connie Riggins and Ms. Rebecca StanCombe for their skillful preparation of various drafts of the monograph. Finally, we express our gratitude and heartfelt thanks to the hundreds of colleagues and students from whom we learned so much about the small college experience—when we were students in a small college, when we served as student affairs staff members in the small college setting, and as faculty in student affairs preparation programs.

George D. Kuh
Bloomington, IN
November, 1985

Andrea C. McAleenan
Washington, D.C.
November, 1985

Chapter 1

The Context for Student Affairs Work in Small Colleges

Andrea C. McAleenan and George D. Kuh

This chapter summarizes the general conditions facing institutions of higher education and provides a backdrop against which the role of student affairs in small colleges can be considered. First, the social, economic, and demographic forces impinging on institutions of higher education (IHEs) are discussed with particular emphasis on the small college. Then, an overview of the remaining chapters is provided.

The Context of Higher Education

Small colleges have played an important role in American postsecondary education. Most were founded to prepare church workers and teachers (Palm, 1984). The several hundred small colleges that existed prior to the twentieth century shared certain goals including fostering students' intellectual, social, and religious development. In the early years, the meta goal of the liberal arts college was to stimulate students' search for understanding about the essential harmony of man, society, and nature. "Curricula were heavily flavored with the humanities to promote values-oriented education" (Palm, 1984, p. 49). These and similar goals remain important in contemporary society; indeed, an argument can be advanced that the need for institutions committed to this theme is as great today as at any time in the past (Cleveland, 1985).

Located in both urban and rural areas, small colleges serve students from a broad socio-economic band and a variety of ethnic and racial backgrounds. Some are state-supported, many are privately endowed and affiliated with religious sects. Some are two year schools while many are four year, often residential institutions. Some are wealthy, many are deficit budgeted. Most organize their curriculum around the aims of liberal education but some are known for specialized technical-vocational programs. Some are oversubscribed but many have more than a few available spaces in their entering classes. Most are coeducational, relatively few are single-sex institutions. Many have forged strong bonds with the communities in which they are located by inviting townspeople to attend lectures, theatrical performances, art exhibits, and musical events. Opportunities for study abroad, internships, community service and innovative instructional methods—while not unique to the small college—are quite visible in most institutions. And small liberal arts colleges continue to dominate the list of institutions with alumni earning Ph.D.'s ("Liberal Arts Colleges Rank High in Production of Ph.D.'s," August 7, 1985).

While billions of federal and state tax dollars are required to maintain the system of public education, independent institutions are supported primarily by tuition and gifts from alumni, philanthropic organizations, and individual donors. To absorb independent college enrollments into public institutions would require an additional five billion dollars annually (Hammond, 1984). On almost any index, the small college has contributed to the breadth, flexibility, and diversity of the American higher education system (Bowen, 1983; Carnegie Commission, 1972; Finklestein & Pfinster, 1984).

The Small College at Risk

During the last few decades, some small colleges have deliberately moved away from their original purpose or been forced to revise their missions in response to unpredictable historical events. The Depression, the GI Bill, Sputnik, the Viet Nam conflict, student activism, and inflation have influenced IHEs in different ways; yet not one of these influences could have been anticipated (Bowen, 1983).

New demands created by a rapidly changing, technologically-oriented world have made it difficult for small, liberal arts colleges to deliver what many consider to be important (Cleveland, 1985). Some IHEs have changed practices and policies in response to more heterogeneous cohorts of students desiring a wider range of curricular options than has been traditionally offered by liberal arts institutions (e.g., nursing, business, computing).

But demographic and economic projections suggest all colleges and universities will face critical challenges through the mid-1990s (Breneman & Finn, 1978; Carnegie Foundation, 1979); these challenges will be particularly severe for small colleges. In 1983, full-time enrollment in the 3,280 IHEs in the United States was 9,166,000. More than one-half of IHEs are privately controlled, but an increasing proportion—now approximately 78%—of all college students attend state-supported institutions. Only 215 institutions are single-sex colleges compared with 519 in 1963-64. The 104 men's colleges enroll approximately 23,000 students while 113,000 students attend 111 women's colleges. About 28% of private colleges are Protestant affiliated, 16% are Catholic. A quarter of the private colleges are seminaries or bible colleges (Broyles & Fernandez, 1984; Grant & Snyder, 1983; Plisco & Stern, 1985).

Vocational preferences of college students have shifted from traditional liberal arts disciplines that are characteristic of many small colleges to occupationally oriented majors. Of the 935,000 degrees conferred in 1980-81, only 7.4% of baccalaureate degrees were in English, literature, history, mathematics, modern foreign languages, and physics. Business and management, engineering, health professions, public affairs, and computer and information science accounted for almost 42% of all baccalaureate degrees. Education majors peaked in 1972-73 with 194,000 graduates but by 1980-81 had declined by 44.3% to 108,000. The impending teacher shortage will probably stimulate enrollment increases in teacher education in the next few years (Grant & Snyder, 1983), but some teacher education reform proposals would make it almost impossible for small colleges to stay in the teacher education business.

Two-thirds of all students currently enrolled in college are under the age of 25, and more than 90% are under 35 years of age. But by 1990 more than 50% of students in college will be over 25 and enrolled part-time. Non-white birth rates have been higher than white birth rates for some time, and by 1990 about 25% of the population will be members of a racial or ethnic minority. Yet racial/ethnic minority student enrollments have remained relatively stable since 1980, about 14% of the total enrollment in four year institutions. However, in two year institutions, the percentage of racial/ethnic minorities was about 21% or 2,842,000 full-time students. In fact, the enrollment increases between 1970-83 took place primarily at two year institutions, a product of flexible admission policies and diverse course offerings.

By 1992, the long-predicted decline in the number of 18 year olds is expected to reduce enrollments to about 8,043,000, a decrease of at least 12%. Because the majority of students in independent institutions attend college full-time, the decrease in the number of students attending privately supported IHEs, most of which are small colleges, is expected to be greater than the decline in state-supported institutions.

In 1981, the Council of Independent Colleges (Peck, 1984) analyzed the impact of shifting demographics, federal policy changes, and an unstable economy on small colleges. Respondents indicated six specific concerns: student financial aids, creative financing options to stabilize the revenue base, contingency planning and consolidation of resources and offerings, student recruitment and retention, institutional marketing, and new program development. Although small colleges were perceived to be more vulnerable to public policy shifts than larger, state-supported institutions, Peck concluded that small colleges were uniquely resilient and that many could adapt more easily and probably more quickly to changing conditions in the external environment. In large measure, survival will depend on how well small colleges respond to fiscal challenges.

Both public and private institutions need adequate funding to contribute to a diverse, comprehensive system of higher education. When competing for resources from similar constituencies, small college advancement officers feel they are forced to compete on an unequal basis. For example, many prospective students claim a preference for attending a small independent college; however, because the difference in cost between state-supported and independent institutions is about $7,000 a year, many students are unwilling or unable to pay the difference. Competition for state funds (e.g., monies appropriated to independent colleges for student aid), donors, and prospective students will likely exacerbate the tension between state-supported and independent schools. But because diversity in higher education is important to maintain, the dominant theme emerging in policy makers' discussions of resource allocation is ensuring adequate funding to support various elements of the total higher education system. For example, the small community college is important because of its low cost, accessibility, and diversified curriculum, characteristics that are particularly attractive to students who must combine college and employment with family responsibilities. Similarly, single-sex, denominational, and elite liberal arts colleges have distinct missions and clientele to serve.

Despite resources acquisition pressure, small colleges have proven to be amazingly resilient, and many have been able to adjust to a rapidly changing environment. Some have questioned whether small colleges have adequate planning processes in place to respond to societal pressures, to manage their resources in times of decline or little growth, and to chart their futures with clear, forward vision (Chafee, 1984; Martin, 1984; Peck, 1984). Certainly strategic planning is important. But if the small college is to remain viable into the next decade and beyond, its distinctive nature must be nurtured and more widely communicated.

Values and Culture in the Small College

Higher education scholars have long been interested in the relationship between the environment or campus climate and students' intellectual and social-emotional development. Continuity—faculty and student affairs staff continuously associated with the institution for a long period of time—has been linked to "generativity," the capacity of persons to be supportive, caring, and sharing of their experiences with one another (Kuh, 1981). Quality also seems to be enhanced by interactions with faculty and peers (Pascarella, 1980) which are encouraged in smaller institutions or living-learning units (Astin, 1977; Chickering, 1969). "Most important, quality is a function of a clear, coherent institutional purpose that lends direction to student and faculty efforts toward acquiring an integrated system of knowledge, values, and behaviors," (Kuh, 1981, p. 2).

At the core of every small college with a salient institutional purpose is a community of students, faculty, and staff with an emotional bond to the institution (Deal & Kennedy, 1982; Palm, 1984) created through explicit shared values, heroes, storytellers, and ceremonies unique to that place. From this cultural network emerges an "institutional saga" (Clark, 1972), or story about how the institution came to be what it is in the present. The institutional saga also contains informal rules for how people are to behave—how they work and play together. Failure to adhere to or to promote shared values undermines the influence of the culture. The emotional bonding process is critical to forming a shared vision of the distinctiveness of the institution.

The resiliency of the small college may be linked to the extent to which the college remains true to its "saga" and maintains its distinctive values and rituals. Ceremonial events such as academic convocations, chapel, commencement, the "last lecture" (a faculty member chosen to make a final address to the college community), and homecoming are cultural celebrations that put on display what is important to the college. Such expressive events, the substance and heart of small colleges, are also important for students. "The sense of unity, structure, and coherence for students is important at a time when they are experiencing instability in their own lives. A rich campus culture influences students who are wrestling with the definition of a personal identity, meaning, and purpose in their own lives. Relevant symbols help create stability; too much ambiguity produces meaninglessness" (R. Rood, personal communication, July 23, 1985). Student affairs staff can help students make meaning of the college experience by translating salient aspects of the institutional saga and encouraging students to embrace the institution's core values.

The distinctive small college environment is personified by people fully committed to an institution's mission and programs mediated by a clear, coherent mission. Small colleges, whether independent or state-supported, provide unique curricular options and diversity of choice in a mass system of higher education in the United States, a system that would be more impersonal and uniform without the existence of small institutions. The student affairs staff member's contribution to the small college mission is the subject of this monograph.

Overview of the Monograph

In the following chapters, the role of student affairs staff in championing the small college mission is described, and the similitude between the traditions of liberal learning, such as values formation and holistic student development, and the goals of student affairs work is underscored. Each chapter contains illustrations of student affairs staff contributions to the sense of personalism that pervades the small college campus—from students' relationships with peers, staff, and faculty to the unique contributions of residential life programming. Student affairs staff are portrayed as catalysts who can mobilize the resources of an evolving small college environment to address the dreams, needs, and aspirations of students and to create a high quality living and learning environment consistent with the liberal education goals of the academy.

In Chapter 2, Kent Hawley and George Kuh examine the developmentally powerful nature of the small college using a campus ecology perspective. The psychological size and physical properties of many small colleges coupled with a salient institutional purpose can create unusually potent educational opportunities. Environmental assessment strategies that have been used at several small colleges are described to illustrate how student affairs staff can monitor environmental influences on students' behavior and encourage a higher quality living and learning experience.

The importance of monitoring the external as well as the internal environment has given new meaning to "strategic planning" on college campuses. In Chapter 3, Daryl Smith addresses the role and responsibilities of the student affairs division in providing leadership for institutional planning and research.

Only a few of the elite small colleges will have slack resources in the next decade; student affairs staff will have to be particularly creative in coming years. In Chapter 4, examples are provided of successful programming innovations that maximize the scarce resources typically available. Any of these activities can be adapted to a particular campus setting; in fact, the accomplishments of the contributors to this chapter can make small college campuses exciting places if we do not allow what might be perceived as adversity to dampen enthusiasm, imagination, and ingenuity.

The integrating themes of synergy and values are distinctive characteristics of most small colleges. In Chapter 5, Robert Young describes these aspects of the small college environment in a positive but not idealistic tone. Young underscores the importance of identifying the common core of values to which the institution subscribes and of maximizing the synergistic opportunities for human development available through interactions with faculty, students, and student affairs staff.

In Chapters 6 and 7, student affairs practitioners join with the editors in describing what it takes to be successful in the small college environment. These chapters have been edited so that multiple contributors speak in one voice to emphasize the remarkable similarity in what they perceived to be the important qualities for effective performance, personal and professional growth, and maintenance of sanity. But, hopefully, the subtle differences in temperament and style across individuals that make our lives and work interesting will be apparent as well.

It should not be surprising that the contributors exhibit enthusiasm for student affairs work in the small college setting. Their positive bias is consistent with findings from recent reports (e.g., Clark, Lotto & Astuto, 1984; Peters & Waterman, 1982) that emphasize the link between a clear sense of purpose, community ethos, and positive affect toward work and indices of achievement. With this in mind, Kuh and McAleenan conclude the monograph by summarizing the major themes that reappear throughout the chapters and offer some suggestions for taking advantage of conditions that bode well for the future of student affairs work in small colleges.

References

Astin, A. W. (1977). *Four critical years.* San Francisco, CA: Jossey-Bass.

Bowen, H. R. (October, 1983). Address to the Association of Independent Colleges and Universities in Massachusetts and Chief Executive Officers of Public Colleges and Universities in Massachusetts. Worcester, MA: College of the Holy Cross.

Breneman, D. W., & Finn, C. E. (Eds.) (1978). *Public policy and private higher education.* Washington, D. C.: Brookings Institute.

Broyles, S. G., & Fernandez, R. M. (1984). *Education directory: Colleges and universities 1983-84.* Washington, D. C.: National Center for Education Statistics.

Carnegie Commission (1972). *The more effective use of resources: An imperative for higher education.* New Jersey: McGraw-Hill.

Carnegie Council on Policy Studies in Higher Education, (1979). *Fair practices in higher education: Rights and responsibilities of students and their colleges in a period of intensified competition for enrollments.* San Francisco: Jossey-Bass.

Chaffee, E. E. (1984). Successful strategic management in small private colleges. *Journal of Higher Education, 55,* 212-241.

Chickering, A. W. (1969). *Education and identity.* San Francisco, CA: Jossey-Bass.

Clark, B. R. (1972). The organizational saga in higher education. *Administrative Science Quarterly, 17,* 178-184.

Clark, D. L., Lotto, L. S., & Astuto, T. A. (1984). Effective schools and school improvement: A comparative analysis of two lines of inquiry. *Educational Administration Quarterly, 20,* 41-68.

Cleveland, H. (1985). Educating for the information society. *Change, 17* (4), 13-21.

Deal, T. E., & Kennedy, A. A. (1982). *Corporate cultures: The rites and rituals of corporate life.* Reading, Massachusetts: Addison-Wesley.

Finkelstein, M. J., & Pfinster, A. O. (1984). The liberal arts college: Managing adaptation to the 1980's. *Journal of Higher Education, 55,* 243-268.

Grant, W. V., & Snyder, T. D. (1983). *Digest of education: Education statistics 1983-84.* Washington, D. C.: National Center for Education Statistics.

Hammond, M. F. (1984). Survival of small private colleges. *Journal of Higher Education, 55,* 360-388.

Kuh, G. D. (1981). *Indices of quality in the undergraduate experience.* AAHE-ERIC/ Higher Education Research Report No. 4. Washington, D.C.: American Association for Higher Education.

"Liberal Arts Colleges Rank High in Production of Ph.D.'s." (August 7, 1985). *The Chronicle of Higher Education,* p. 3.

Martin, W. B. (1984). Adaptation and distinctiveness. *Journal of Higher Education, 55,* 286-296.

Palm, R. L. (1984). Student personnel administration at the small college. *NASPA Journal, 22* (2), 48-54.

Pascarella, E. T. (1980). Student-faculty informal contact and college outcomes. *Review of Educational Research, 50,* 545-595.

Peck, R. (1984). Entrepreneurship as a significant factor in successful adaptation. *Journal of Higher Education, 55,* 269-285.

Peters, T. J., & Waterman, R. H. (1982). *In search of excellence: Lessons from America's best run companies.* New York: Harper & Row.

Plisco, V. W., & Stern, J. D. (Eds.) (1985). *The condition of education, 1985 edition.* Washington, D. C.: National Center for Education Statistics.

Chapter 2

The Small College as a Developmentally Powerful Learning Environment

Kent T. Hawley and George D. Kuh

Compared with students at large universities, students at small colleges tend to be more altruistic, are more involved in campus governance, are more likely to take part in classroom discussions, and have more opportunities to assume leadership roles and to participate in athletics, journalism, and theatre (Astin, 1977). Other research suggests that students at small colleges evidence higher academic achievement (Baird, 1969), and usually perceive the campus environment as friendlier, more cohesive, more group-oriented, and less competitive than their counterparts at large institutions (Walsh, 1978). After considering the findings of numerous studies of student development, Astin (1977) concluded: "the proliferation of large institutions during the past twenty years has reduced the students' chances of being involved in campus life and of being on close terms with the faculty" (p. 245).

Why is it that small college environments seem to be "developmentally powerful?" In this chapter, Blocher's (1978) campus ecology model is used to illuminate conditions common to many small colleges that encourage human development. Examples are then provided to illustrate how ecological principles have been used by student affairs staff in several small colleges in designing policies and practices that take advantage of opportunities for growth and development inherent in the small college setting.

Elements of the Small College Ecology

Within the last decade, it has become clear that what happens to students during college cannot simply be attributed to their biographical, intellectual, or psycho-social characteristics *or* to institutional resources such as faculty, library holdings, and athletic facilities. A more powerful way to account for what happens to students during college is to focus on the *transactions* between persons (students, faculty, student affairs staff, peers) *and* the environment (Levin, 1936), however defined. For example, a college campus can be defined in terms of physical properties, dominant student subcultures (Clark & Trow, 1966), personality or ambience reflected by the interests and characteristics of the majority of students (Astin & Holland, 1961), and expectations for behavior or environmental "press" (Stern, 1970). These perspectives are encompassed within the concept of campus "ecology," i.e., the reciprocal interactions and relationships between individuals, groups of students, and institutional agents *and* the environment of the college. In this formulation, students' behavior is a function of students' characteristics *interacting* with a college environment made up of physical spaces, policies, and people (Huebner, 1979).

Drawing upon theory and empirical research, Blocher (1974, 1978) constructed a model of an optimal learning environment comprised of three major subsystems: (1) the opportunity subsystem, (2) the support subsystem, and (3) the reward subsystem.

The Opportunity Subsystem

Striking similarities exist among insitutions in the organization and administration of academic and student life programs. For example, most colleges have social programming bodies, intramural and intercollegiate athletic teams, numerous curricular and co-curricular clubs, and one or more campus governance structures that invite or require student representation. On residential campuses, living units afford additional opportunities for student leadership and participation in formal and informal projects undertaken by the living unit.

Because many of the same kinds of maintenance functions or standing patterns of behavior common to large institutions of higher education (IHEs) are also required on the small campus, students at small colleges can usually become involved in campus activities with less effort than might be the case in many larger institutions. Behavior setting theory (Barker, 1960) suggests that an inverse relationship exists between the number of people on the campus and the frequency and intensity of opportunities or "forces that impinge upon these people," (Walsh, 1978, p. 7). Following this argument, the small college environment can be described as an underpopulated setting. In underpopulated settings, "people tend to be busier, more vigorous, more versatile, and more involved" (Walsh, 1978, p. 7), and are usually encouraged to become involved in a variety of activities. In larger IHEs, specialization is often expected, particularly in faculty or student affairs positions.

For optimum learning and development to occur through students' involvement in these activities, students must be challenged to think about whether their behavior is compatible with their goals and the institution's purpose. Students benefit most through active participation when the college has a clearly explicated system of values—communicated by institutional agents—within which students can think about, reflect on, and continually integrate their experiences.

The role of the student affairs staff on an underpopulated campus is to establish and encourage students to help maintain an infra-structure that provides developmental experiences for students. Many small colleges use students extensively as peer counselors, residence hall staff, and members of programming committees. A campus judicial board system that involves students at various levels—from residence hall bodies to campus judicial councils including faculty and administrators—is a powerful opportunity subsystem. Student affairs staff can maximize the opportunities associated with judicial board hearings by encouraging students serving on and appearing before these bodies to reflect on what they have learned from the judicial board process.

Both the physical and the organizational structures of residence halls can enhance positive learning experiences. In general, small colleges tend to have a higher percentage of students living in residence halls or other kinds of group living situations. Small colleges can create more individualized residential units, less subject to the systematization required when dealing with large numbers of students. Experiments with roommate matching, peer governance models, and room or hallway personalization are sometimes easier to implement in the less bureaucratized small college (Schroeder, Anchors & Jackson, 1978; Schroeder, Nicholls & Kuh, 1983). One study of learning environments on a small campus (Damier, 1978) confirmed that students in an older hall with wide hallways and a "town meeting" organizational structure perceived significantly greater congruence between their "ideal" of residential life and their actual experiences than did students in more modern, traditionally organized living units.

Opportunity subsystems not only provide an avenue for student involvement but also can be advantageous to an understaffed student affairs unit. For example, students can be expected to manage and enforce campus parking policies with a student affairs staff member in an advisory role. Policies developed and then modified with the help of student members on a peer "hearing board" can relieve both harried campus security staff and administrators from regular confrontations with student violators. Furthermore, a policy that requires students to confront violators (peers) is an excellent educational device to encourage responsible behavior. For such an approach to be successful, some training for students who agree to administer these policies should be provided by student affairs staff.

Student government can create an opportunity for interaction among students, faculty, and administrators. The prestige of student government may be further enhanced if students take their governing responsibilities seriously, and when faculty committees and administrators seek its advice on policy changes. By taking student government seriously the institution reaffirms the importance of students. The opportunity for dialogue with faculty encourages students to think beyond planning social events and to become more involved in the academic life of the institution. A student body president once admonished faculty for pursuing departmental special interests at the expense of the total institution and subsequently influenced the faculty's vote for higher academic standards. Without a vehicle to encourage such exchanges, students and faculty may be deprived of beneficial learning opportunities.

Small colleges have many advantages, but they are not necessarily ideal or perfect environments. For example, it is unlikely that students attending small colleges are challenged to a greater degree than are their counterparts at larger institutions. In fact, the *novelty* of challenges may be greater on a large university campus if one's peers are more heterogeneous in terms of background and preferred lifestyles. Also, in a large university environment expectations are more likely to be ambiguous and behavior standards are less likely to be mediated by a coherent sense of values or institutional purposes requiring a higher level of cognitive complexity to handle the *abstractness* of what is expected by institutional agents and influential peers. But the *intensity* of challenges encountered by students in small colleges may be as great or greater than those encountered by university students because anonymity is difficult to maintain among faculty and peers in an underpopulated setting.

To realize the potential of the small college opportunity subsystem, a clear, coherent set of values, from which the expectations for students' behavior can be derived, is needed. Of course, smallness alone is not necessarily associated with a salient purpose. A clearly articulated institutional mission implies that the college community "has an ideal or vision . . . expectations of what its members are to become. Such ideals or expectations, so out of fashion these days, may be more silent than vocal; they may work their effects out of awareness; they may constitute the invisible college . . . and when such expectations are consistently expressed in all structures and activities of the institution [they] mutually reinforce one another . . . it is the coherence, the consistency, the 'atmosphere' . . . that makes its impact on [students'] development" (Heath, 1968, p. 243).

The Support Subsystem

Blocher suggested that a developmentally powerful learning environment provides students with *structure* and *support* enabling them to deal with the ambiguous, complex, abstract, and novel situations encountered during college that demand responses beyond the student's repertoire. Support is provided through accessibility and active involvement of responsible adult and significant peer role models who participate in students' interpersonal networks, and who regularly provide empathy, caring, and nurturance for students. During periods of emotional crises or physical need, support may be in the form of formal structures such as peer advisors or trained staff in counseling or health centers. On a daily basis, support is manifested through informal, almost tacit understandings and communications with peers, and serendipitous, unplanned contacts with caring, nurturing student affairs staff and faculty.

Small colleges are almost ideal for encouraging informal "circles of support"—through student and professional residence hall staff, concerned faculty and administrators, and campus support services such as counseling, health, and career development services. However, the potential educational impact of these networks is often not fully realized.

The importance of providing support is clearly evident in students' concerns about room assignments and roommates. The residence hall is a student's "home" and a source of security. A peer support system within which members are well known usually develops in most small institutions. Peer support was gratefully expressed by one student who said, "When my grandmother died, the whole floor cried with me."

A career development office employs peer counselors responsible for interviewing every new student, beginning with those who identify themselves as "undecided." This early personal contact provides another source of support for new students whose anxieties are often exacerbated by the common question, "What is your major?" The well-trained peer counselor can not only introduce the new student to the career development process, but can make referrals of students who have additional concerns.

Peers can obtain support through programming groups traditionally involved in organized student groups, all-campus festivals such as homecoming, and weekly social events. Student committees can also provide support in areas such as the health services' promotion of healthy life styles. On some campuses students design and implement alcohol education programs, and organize support groups such as ALANON and Alcoholics Anonymous. Peer support and programming groups have been especially valuable in assisting older non-traditional students in their transition to college life. Peer monitoring also has proven helpful to students with marginal high school records or to those who have put special interests such as athletics or music above academic performance. At one school, monitoring athletes' academic performance by peers resulted in a 90% eligibility rate, a substantial increase over previous monitoring schemes.

The physical dimensions of most small colleges increases the likelihood that students see and interact with a wide range of faculty at concerts, plays, athletic events, meals, and other out-of-class events and, therefore, are regularly exposed to appropriate behavior in different kinds of settings. The power of the small college support system is not a function of the number of formal, institutionalized support services. Rather, any advantage lies in the greater accessibility and availability of responsible faculty and student affairs staff with whom students are involved beyond the classroom.

The Reward Subsystem

Blocher (1978) hypothesized that for optimal levels of learning, students must receive *feedback* about their performance relative to the expectations of the campus community. Also important are opportunities to experiment with and to *apply* newly acquired behaviors in problem-solving, decision-making, and relations with peers, faculty, and student affairs staff. The work of Chickering (1969) and other psycho-social theorists (e.g., Marcia, 1966; Loevinger, 1976) can be used to identify behaviors (e.g., assertiveness) associated with core developmental tasks (e.g., competence) that must be mastered for students to move on to more advanced developmental tasks.

While the concept of integrating experiences was introduced under the opportunities subsystem, for students to optimally benefit, integration must occur across all three subsystems. That is, student affairs staff and faculty must go out of their way to challenge, reward, and support students in reflecting on what is happening to them and to encourage acquisition and integration of new behaviors consonant with the expectations of the college.

On the small college campus, rewards often come quickly and easily. While only the highly recruited and talented high school athletic stars receive recognition in larger universities, a student doesn't have to be an exceptional athlete to participate on some small college varsity teams. The same conditions apply to almost all other activities and areas of involvement. Typically, students who make special efforts in each department and in each class receive recognition by faculty, peers, and student affairs staff.

However, since most people know each other on a small campus, negative feedback comes quickly as well. The campus "grapevine" carries news more quickly than does the weekly student newspaper. A student who has academic problems, who drinks too much, or who isn't attending classes is soon identified, and can be confronted and supported to modify his or her behavior. The lack of anonymity is a mixed blessing; although rewards are closely tied to behavior, and questionable behavior can be identified quickly, a less than desirable reputation is difficult to change.

Most colleges have recognition systems built into the rituals and traditions of campus life. Academic achievement is constantly reinforced through announcement of scholarship recipients and publication of Deans' Lists. High performing students are invited to serve as tutors, laboratory assistants, and peer academic advisors. In this sense, honors convocations, athletic banquets, newspaper publicity, and appointments to honor societies are all a part of the reward system.

A summary of college achievements appears on the placement resumes prepared by seniors seeking employment after graduation. In a small school, more students can often demonstrate involvement and accomplishment in more than one area and can document leadership skills and experience, all of which usually positively influences a potential employer. Offers of employment to senior students can be reinterpreted as incentives for underclassmen. The commencement program listing those graduating with honors is available for all to see. Since students are known as individuals by most members of the campus community, recognition is widely shared and reinforced.

The small college environment is uniquely suited for providing opportunities for feedback, application, and on-going integration. As mentioned earlier, few students can remain anonymous on a small college campus; therefore, appropriate behavior can be almost immediately reinforced, and inappropriate behavior can be challenged. Likewise, because of the "underpopulated" nature of most small college campuses, students have numerous opportunities to apply or experiment with different forms of more acceptable behavior, and can apply and integrate these new ideas and behaviors through participation in class-related and co-curricular activities.

Blocher's model is but one conceptual framework that student affairs staff can use to encourage a developmentally powerful living and learning environment. Elements of other theoretical frameworks and conceptual models can be used in concert with Blocher's model to structure discussions about how to maximize the opportunities inherent in the small college environment for intellectual and social-emotional development. The next section contains illustrations of how Blocher's concepts have been used on small college campuses within the ecosystem design and implementation model.

Ecosystem Assessment and the Design of Campus Subsystems

"Ecosystem theory" is based on the early work of Kaiser (1973) who studied how college students are influenced by physical and psychological surroundings. Kaiser's studies led to the establishment of a task force to improve mental health services (WICHE, 1973). Later, ecosystem design strategies were applied to college campuses (Aulepp & Delworth, 1976; Banning, 1978; Huebner, 1979).

The ecosystem assessment and design process is especially applicable to small colleges with overworked but "underpopulated" offices. The approach is simple, but requires that persons responsible for implementing environmental interventions be involved in the design process. This creates a psychological bonding between assessment results and those persons in a position to influence change.

Every campus has a "design" or environment which shapes and influences students. In that sense, the small college campus can be viewed as a total learning environment or "macro-system." It is considerably easier to succeed in modifying a small campus environment than that of a larger institution. However, a "micro-system" approach has been used effectively with subunits at larger campuses (Delworth, Svob, Ford & Hawley, 1975; Huebner, 1979). The ecosystem assessment and design process described in the following pages has been used with modifications at the following small Iowa colleges: Graceland, Waldorf, Clarke, and Wartburg.

Although various planning structures may be employed, it is valuable to work with and through existing structures. An independently organized ecosystem planning committee on one campus was not successful because it failed to relate effectively to the established campus decision making structures. At other campuses, where the student affairs staff and student-faculty policy committees served as initiators, the assessment and planning processes have met with some degree of success.

Eight basic assumptions outlined by Aulepp and Delworth (1976) underlie the "ecosystem" approach:

(1) The campus environment consists of all the stimuli that impinge upon students including physical facilities, biological developmental factors, and social stimuli.

(2) A transactional relationship exists between college students and their campus environment in that students shape the environment and are shaped by the physical setting, social influences, traditions, etc.

(3) The focus of environmental design is shaping properties of the campus environment. Students are viewed as active choice-making agents who may accede to, transform, or nullify environmental influences. Physical environment changes may have a greater impact upon students in small colleges because of the likelihood that a substantial proportion of students may be influenced by such changes.

(4) Every student possesses the capacity for a wide spectrum of possible behaviors. A given campus environment may facilitate or inhibit one or more of these behaviors. To the extent possible, a campus should be intentionally designed to create opportunities, incentives, and rewards for growth and development.

(5) Students will attempt to cope with any educational environment in which they are placed. If students perceive the environment to be incompatible with their values and preferences, the students may react negatively or fail to develop desirable qualities. Some students may avoid a negative environment by withdrawing from school.

(6) Because of the wide range of individual differences among students, "fitting" the campus environment to students requires the creation of a variety of campus sub-environments. There must be an attempt to design for the wide variety of individual characteristics found among students (see Huebner, 1979). The establishment and nurturance of support groups and campus organizations provides a choice of sub-environments.

(7) Every campus has a design, even if the administration, faculty, and students have not planned it or are not consciously aware of it. A design technology for campus environments, therefore, is useful both to identify and analyze existing campus environments and to design new ones.

(8) Successful campus design seems to be linked to involvement of all campus members including students, faculty, staff, administration, and trustees.

The design process, as described by Aulepp and Delworth (1976), can begin at any one of seven steps. Most small colleges have already established institutional statements of purpose reflecting their values and goals. Therefore, we recommend step five, measurement of student perceptions, as a starting point. The seven steps are:

(1) The planning committee, in conjunction with other community members, reviews the educational values implied in the institution's "mission" statement.

(2) Institutional values are translated into specific goals to give direction to the planning process. This is a difficult part of the design process, since goals tend to be general and difficult to translate into action. A workshop on how to translate values into working goals can be helpful at this stage of planning.

(3) Campus environments are designed or modified to provide systems, processes, and activities to achieve important goals. It sometimes helps to outline specific objectives, such as increasing minority student enrollment and retention by 10% or reducing damage in the residence halls by a certain amount.

(4) Environments are modified to respond to students' needs and preferences. Institutional changes do not usually come easy. But, through perseverance and commitment to the institutional saga, changes can take place. Residence halls can be converted to co-educational units. Billing procedures can be changed and orientation programs restructured, library hours extended, etc. Academic calendars, vacation schedules, and social scheduling can be changed to encourage attainment of stated academic and social goals.

(5) Student perceptions of the environments are measured using a macro-campus approach. Both objective and anecdotal responses should be elicited. The planning committee should include questions that deal with specific concerns of various campus constituencies.

(6) Student behavior related to environmental perceptions is monitored. Records of damage reports in the residence halls, withdrawals from school, discipline cases, and attendance and behavior at social, cultural, and athletic events can be systematically monitored.

(7) Designers review data reflecting student perceptions and behavior to learn more about student/environment fit and to subsequently "design" more appropriate environments. The planning committee on a small campus has access to a "grapevine" of information which provides early, continual feedback, even without formal measurements. However, objective perceptions collected on a systematic basis may discourage emotional reactions to issues and provide a rational and objective basis for planning.

Tactics for Designing and Implementing Campus Interventions

An easy way to get started is to select a standardized survey instrument covering a broad range of campus services that allows inclusion of specific campus-related questions. The American College Testing Service *Student Opinion Survey* (1979) has proven to be a useful instrument. It provides for 30 optional questions in addition to the standard questions for which national norms are available. The availability of normative data permits a college to measure the perceptions of its students against those of similar institutions.

One of the most useful aspects of this ecosystem approach is that it provides a method for collecting specific student comments often called "ERs," an abbreviation for "environmental referents." Such anecdotal comments provide information which can guide decisions on how to improve the campus environment. One popular approach is to ask students to identify the five items on the survey instrument most important to them and then to complete an "ER" form requesting specific comments. A typical ER form looks like this:

STEP 1	STEP 2	STEP 3	STEP 4
Statement Number	What things in the environment exist or have happened to make you feel this way?	How have you responded to this situation or feeling?	What should be done to change the environment to improve the situation?

The "ER" form is valuable for several reasons.

(1) It identifies those items of greatest concern to students. The objective or rating portion of the survey provides average scores for all items, but these mean scores do not differentiate among more or/less important items.

(2) The items that received the highest number of "ER" responses can be placed in rank order and compared from year to year to give a rough priority ordering of student concerns.

(3) The "ERs" provide specific recommendations which can provide a basis for planning and action.

(4) The "ERs" have high face validity for students.

The objective survey produces an average score and standard deviation of all items broken down by categories designated by the campus planning staff. The total group average can be separated by sex, class, residence units, transfers, etc. It is thus possible to identify the groups that register satisfaction or dissatisfaction with particular items. The objective survey instrument tends to elicit more balanced responses with the negative ratings balancing the positive. The average of the ratings permits a comparison with the rating at similar institutions, since forms like the ACT *Student Opinion Survey* are nationally normed.

The comments from the "ER" form allow an anecdotal elaboration on the items of greatest concern to students. Some of the comments may be quite specific about recommended changes or the performance of staff members. Such comments may disturb a sensitive administrator, since the "ER" form is designed to elicit primarily negative responses.

But ER responses may also point to possible solutions. For example, at one campus, "ER" comments about a food service were negative, yet on the survey instrument the food service was rated high, significantly higher than those of other institutions. The "ER" comments helped to clarify that while the food and service were good, the meal refund policy was considered confusing and unfair. On another campus, parking was listed as the number one concern. However, it became clear that the issue was not availability of parking but the need for more security, better lighting, and a more effective method of snow removal.

These concerns were satisfactorily addressed with very little cost to the college.

Benefits of Campus Design Interventions

Student affairs staff are often so busy attending to the daily demands of the job that their perspective of what the college is trying to accomplish becomes inadvertently compromised. The campus design process, grounded in an ecological framework, encourages staff to periodically consider annual goals, objectives and attainments within the overall mission of the college. Routine tasks seem to have greater meaning when recognized as consistent with and integral to attaining broad institutional goals.

The ecosystem survey process puts campus life under the conscious scrutiny of students as well as staff. If the survey results are shared as soon as possible, students know that their concerns are being taken seriously. For successful interventions to be initiated, both the summary of the survey and the specific "ER" responses should be reviewed with key administrators for their use in planning. The survey originating "design committee" should review all of the results to determine which interventions should be given priority.

In addition to assessing operational structures, improving support systems, and providing significant rewards for appropriate behavior, the ecosystem planning process provides valuable aid for establishing specific objectives. The priority list of student concerns can serve as a basis for joint planning sessions between the student affairs staff and student government leaders. Candidates for student leadership positions often incorporate suggestions from the survey into their platforms and use them as a basis for setting objectives. Institutional support staff—custodians, food service employees, and secretaries—typically look forward to the feedback they get from the survey.

Below are some illustrative interventions that have been successful in responding to typical problems linked to the campus environment.

A male residence hall regarded as an "animal house" and a women's hall known as "the convent," were converted to coeducational units based on "ER" data. The interventions met with early resistance by some students, but gratifying results were realized in just one year as reflected by survey data: residence hall damages were reduced 43% and retention improved significantly. The two major interventions were (a) to convert single sex halls to co-educational units, and (b) to replace a traditional housemother-houseparent staff with master's level hall counselors. The staffing change shifted the emphasis more from that of control to that of a student-centered living environment. Although the interventions probably were not the only factors associated with desirable changes in damage and retention rates, the actions taken were clearly linked in some manner to the improvement in the residence hall environment.

On another campus, ER data were used to rearrange the class schedule to eliminate a "free" day in the middle of the week that encouraged midweek partying, a non-productive, irritating distraction. The elimination of the free day and an increased number of social events scheduled for weekends improved the social climate and reduced the number of students leaving the campus on weekends. At the same college, creative social programming alternatives to beer parties and bar hopping resulted in a 50% decrease in beer consumption by members of a fraternity who appointed recreation majors as social programmers and promoted a series of theme parties.

Soliciting responses from international and minority students can increase campus awareness about their unique perspectives and concerns. Employment of minority and international students as academic tutors and laboratory instructors can help break down negative stereotypes. Interaction between black, international, and traditional students was enhanced on one campus through cooperation on common projects such as fashion shows, coffee houses and a community service effort. Orientation group leaders from diverse racial and ethnic groups provide alternative role models for new students as well as strengthen the bonds between the orientation group leaders and the institution.

Conclusion

The small college can be thought of as a living-learning ecology that provides numerous opportunities for student involvement, support and encouragement for risk-taking, experimentation with new behaviors, and almost immediate feedback and recognition to students. Every campus is a unique environment, open to some degree of influence, and the educative role of student affairs staff can be enhanced through adoption of an ecologically-based design process that identifies targets for interventions. The campus design process provides a framework for (1) thinking about the small college campus as a developmentally powerful learning environment, (2) comparing the current campus environment with the desired institutional context, and (3) identifying actions that are responsive to students' needs and concerns. Systematic assessment of students' perceptions and behavior, using the campus ecology perspective described here, has resulted in positive outcomes at several small colleges, and can be modified for use at most institutions.

References

ACT Student Opinion Survey. (1979). Iowa City, IA: ACT College Testing Program.

Astin, A. W. (1977). *Four critical years.* San Francisco, CA: Jossey-Bass.

Astin, A. W., & Holland, J. L. (1961). The environmental assessment technique: A way to measure college environments. *Journal of Educational Psychology, 52,* 308-316.

Aulepp, L., & Delworth, U. (1976). *Training manual for an ecosystem model.* Boulder, CO: WICHE.

Banning, J. H. (Ed.). (1978). *Campus ecology: A perspective for student affairs.* Cincinnati, OH: National Association of Student Personnel Administrators.

Barker, R. G. (1968). *Ecological psychology: Concepts and methods for studying the environment of human behavior.* Stanford, CA: Stanford University Press.

Baird, L. L. (1969). Big school, small school: A critical examination of the hypothesis. *Journal of Educational Psychology, 60,* 253-260.

Blocher, D. H. (1974). Toward an ecology of student development. *Personnel and Guidance Journal, 52,* 360-365.

Blocher, D. H. (1978). Campus learning environments and the ecology of student development. In J. Banning (Ed.), *Campus ecology: A perspective for student affairs* (pp. 17-23). Cincinnati, OH: National Association of Student Personnel Administrators.

Clark, B. R., & Trow, M. (1966). The organizational context. In T. M. Newcomb and E. K. Wilson (Eds.), *College peer groups: Problems and prospects for research* (pp. 17-70). Chicago, IL: Aldine.

Damier, B. (1978). *The measurement and structuring of residence hall environments.* Waverly, IA: Wartburg College.

Delworth, U., Svob, R., Ford, M., & Hawley, K. (1975). Designing campus ecosystems. *NASPA Journal, 13* (1), 40-44.

Heath, D. H. (1968). *Growing up in college.* San Francisco, CA: Jossey-Bass.

Huebner, L. A. (Ed.). (1979). Redesigning campus environments. *New Directions for Student Services,* No. 6. San Francisco, CA: Jossey-Bass.

Kuh, G. D. (1981). *Indices of quality in the undergraduate experience.* AAHE-ERIC/ Higher Education Resarch Report No. 4. Washington, D.C.: American Association for Higher Education.

Kaiser, L. R. (July, 1973). *The ecosystem design process applied to the emotional problems of college students.* Presented at the Seventh Annual Workshop Concerning Emotional Problems of College Students, Greeley, Colorado.

Levin, K. (1936). *Principles of topological psychology.* New York: McGraw-Hill.

Loevinger, J. (1976). *Ego development: Conceptions and theories.* San Francisco, CA: Jossey-Bass.

Marcia, J. (1966). Development and validation of ego-identity status. *Journal of Personality and Social Psychology, 35,* 551-558.

Schroeder, C. C., Anchors, S., & Jackson, S. (1978). *Making yourself at home.* Cincinnati, OH: American College Personnel Association.

Schroeder, C. C., Nicholls, G. E., & Kuh, G. D. (1983). Exploring the rain forest: Testing assumptions and taking risks. In G. D. Kuh (Ed.), Understanding student affairs organizations. *New Directions for Student Services,* No. 23 (pp. 51-65). San Francisco: Jossey-Bass.

Stern, G. C. (1970). *People in context.* New York, NY: Wiley.

Walsh, W. B. (1978). Person/environment interaction. In J. Banning (Ed.), *Campus ecology: A perspective for student affairs* (pp. 6-16). Cincinnati, OH: National Association of Student Personnel Administrators.

Western Interstate Commission on Higher Education (1973). *The ecosystem model: Designing campus environments.* Boulder, CO: Western Interstate Commission on Higher Education.

Chapter 3

The Role of Student Affairs in Planning and Institutional Research

Daryl G. Smith

Systematic planning and institutional research are important to small colleges grappling with the challenges of retrenchment brought on by demographic shifts and financial instability (Peterson, 1985). Yet, because of limited resources and staff, small colleges often do little systematic planning and research.

This chapter provides an overview of the role the student affairs division can play in assisting, shaping, and informing an institutional planning and research agenda. The presentation is organized to respond to three questions central to institutional planning and research:

1. What should the planning and research program look like?

2. What role should student affairs professionals play?

3. How can the tasks be accomplished with limited staff and resources?

Strategic Planning

Planning is a process by which an institution articulates goals, outlines means of achieving these goals, and then oversees implementation. For many authors planning is viewed as an empirically based, rational process. Heydinger (1980) described planning as "a process that builds on available evidence and attempts to embrace the future through rational decision-making" (p. 2). This definition emphasizes the connection between institutional research and planning; institutional research can, if done properly, be designed to inform decisions about the future which institutions must make and to provide a basis for creating a climate of change. However, other writers appropriately caution that planning is not just a rational process but a human and political one as well (Bean & Kuh, 1984; Cope, 1981; Keller, 1983; Peters & Waterman, 1982; Steiner & Miner, 1977).

The current literature on planning makes a potentially important distinction between "long range planning," the phrase of a decade ago, and "strategic planning" (Yavitz & Newman, 1982). For years, an institution's planning goal was to develop a five or ten year plan that could be written up and supposedly used as a guide during that period. These plans often depicted the institution's present situation and projected a likely future from that base. In contrast, strategic planning differs in at least four ways in preparing an institution for the future:

1. Strategic planning emphasizes, to a much more significant degree, the internal and external environments influencing the institution. Information is gathered about competition from institutions in the same market segment, institutional strengths and weaknesses, and general external environmental conditions (e.g., demographic shifts, economic conditions, federal policy). These data are carefully studied and included in generating alternative "likely scenarios." As Keller (1983) has noted, "strategic planning is an attempt to give organizations antennae to sense the changing environment" (p. vii).

2. Strategic planning does not make single-minded assumptions about the future. Often, strategic planners will outline a number of possibilities so that the institution can choose among and deal creatively with possibilities. Moreover, because strategic plan-

ning is a continuing, emergent process, the institution is not bound by a single concept of the future. As Cope (1981) suggested, "strategic planning assumes an open system in which organizations are dynamic and changing" (p. 4).

3. Strategic planning does not necessarily produce a single document of a "long-range plan." Emphasis is given to producing action rather than a report.

4. Because process is emphasized, strategic planning takes into account political issues as well as rational and empirical perspectives (Bean & Kuh, 1984; Keller, 1983).

Because strategic planning is dynamic and responsive to changes in the internal and external environments, a strategic approach to planning is inferred when planning is discussed in this paper.

Planning and Student Affairs

Planning and research needs within small colleges present a unique opportunity for student affairs to play a significant role in enhancing institutional quality. First, because small colleges tend to be student-centered, much of the information needed today to identify and respond to major issues in institutional planning involve present and prospective students. Enrollments and factors that affect enrollments require information that student affairs staff can provide; e.g., the numbers of students who persist to graduation, the institution's strengths and weaknesses as perceived by prospective and current students, why students stay and leave, and alumni attainments. Student affairs departments have access to both quantitative and qualitative information of this kind and should be a major source of information for the planning process.

Second, many student affairs professionals, by training and inclination, are process-oriented. We are not only concerned about the content of a decision, but also about how decisions are made. Strategic planning requires good decisions and subsequent action consistent with decisions. Toward these ends, a strategic planning process must be appropriate to the institution and to the issues. Student affairs staff spend a good part of their time advising groups on how to improve the quality of their decisions, how to involve the proper constituencies in the decision-making process, and on how to communicate decisions to the larger community. A similar process orientation is essential to effective planning. Communication is vital and, as Young (Chapter 5) suggested, the small college setting makes such discussions easier to schedule. These activities have been central to student affairs work, and we should seize the opportunity to lend our expertise to the entire institution.

Third, student affairs work in small colleges provides a view of the entire institution and its impact on students. This holistic institutional perspective combined with a developmental and holistic view of students makes the student affairs perspective essential to good planning in today's higher education environment.

However, influencing the direction of an institution depends on many factors. Fundamental to the success of an influential student affairs program is its identification with the mission of the institution (Smith, 1975). To the degree that student affairs professionals are perceived to understand and to promote the purposes of the institution, other institutional agents will be open to actively involving student affairs staff in the planning process. Because small college chief student affairs officers often participate on cabinet level and other institutional decision-making bodies, the potential exists for effective leadership.

Beginning a program of research to address *existing* issues of institutional concern can also provide an opportunity for student affairs participation in planning and for the role of student-based research in the planning process. Student affairs staff should investigate those issues that have direct links between the institution's concern for the future and the needs and concerns of current students. For example, as McAleenan and Kuh (Chapter 1) indicated, enrollment stability promises to remain an important issue in many small colleges in the coming decade. Retention is another area that can be the responsibility of student affairs and is also central to institutional planning and stability. Student affairs staff are in the best position to take the initiative in these areas. In institutions where research and planning are not underway, their importance and potential must be demonstrated. Identifying an area of concern (e.g., enrollment) and showing how research information can be useful is a good way to begin.

Before embarking on a research project, it is important to look at the existing or potential planning agenda for the institution. To be useful, research must address real issues or concerns. Knowledge about the institution's planning agenda is essential to good research. The following agenda for planning provides an outline useful both for the purpose of student affairs in a particular institutional context and for the institution:

1. Articulate issues, needs, and problems as defined from the institutional perspective. Planning and research cannot deal with all possible questions and concerns; therefore, only the most pressing of those that are linked to institutional stability should be pursued. Priority issues can be identified through "environmental scanning," or looking beyond the institution to the external factors that may have an impact on its future (Morrison, Renfro & Boncher, 1984). The process of clarifying institutional priorities not only makes planning more manageable, it also increases the probability that the process, the data collected, and the results will be taken seriously. This is a time when the student affairs professional should focus on the institution and its external environment, not on his or her own agenda for the institution.

2. Analyze the values, traditions, and characteristics of the institution which play an important role in how the college is defined and functions. This is an important element in any planning process but is particularly important in the small college where institutional climate and institutional values are likely to be more central than they are at larger institutions. A strategic planning process which focuses too much on

external considerations may embark on strategies that will not succeed because they fail to take into account the traditions, values, and mission of the institution. Indeed, as McAleenan and Kuh suggested (Chapter 1), recognizing the central character of the institution is essential to survival.

3. Develop alternative "likely scenarios" of the college's future including enrollment, nature of the student body, financial conditions, etc., and institutional responses to these "scenarios." One of the interesting challenges in strategic planning is to picture the future without being co-opted by a single image of the future. Predicting the future is fraught with problems and mapping a single strategy to reach a single goal might well be shortsighted. Commitment to a single approach is usually not required; the process will change as the future unfolds. However, we can plan for what is needed or will be needed. As Kerr (1980) noted: "It is better to plan to meet the future effectively than just to fear it as a new dark age . . . The future is not fully determined in advance. It will be substantially affected by what institutions and individuals decide to do" (pp. 6-7).

4. Make the process as efficient as possible. Opportunities for participation can be provided without wasting participants' time. It is important to identify those goals or plans about which there is significant institutional or departmental consensus. In these areas, an elaborate process for decision-making may not be required; however, an appropriate structure and personnel will be needed to implement the plan. On issues about which significant disagreement exists, all the necessary constituencies should be involved and enough time provided for deliberation. For example, if there is disagreement about the impact of changing demographics of the college, groups of faculty, students, administrators, and alumni might be brought together to consider the available data and

make recommendations. Developing an elaborate process to consider all issues, regardless of perceived importance or degree of consensus, makes the planning process seem to be a waste of time. Those making judgments about the college must have a realistic picture of the institution and be sensitive to prevalent views. Student affairs staff must be willing to listen carefully to other constituencies as well as to students. Listening is an important element in establishing a credible planning process and a responsive, useful, usable plan. Consultation skills are required (Powers & Powers, 1983) and make it possible to learn the issues, determine if disagreement exists, and which issues require attention. Consultation also provides opportunities for others to influence institutional decision-making.

5. Tailor the planning process to particular institutional styles and culture. Decision-making occurs in the context of accepted ways of proceeding. Some colleges require more participation by all constituent groups that might be affected by a decision. Others expect adherence to more narrowly defined areas of responsibility in which the faculty or the administration or the board are expected to play primary roles in decision-making. The institution's norms must be understood and used if the planning agenda is to produce action-oriented decisions. Planning cannot and should not be an excuse for nonaction.

Institutional Research

An effective program of institutional research can create openness to change in the institution by providing an impetus for effective planning and by providing information to decision-makers. For example, at one college, information about declining applicant pools was shared in a way that got the attention of faculty and senior administrators. That research prompted significant attention to a market analysis of the institution. The planning which followed had a dramatic, positive impact on the institution's admissions picture. At another institution, providing student retention data to the faculty, and the relationship of retention rates, admission selectivity, and the budget resulted in comprehensive curriculum revisions. An institutional research program can respond to the concerns within student affairs while also addressing institutional concerns, but it must be implemented in ways that can be used and understood throughout the college. In small colleges, one department does have the potential to influence the direction of the institution. Good research on areas relating to student affairs can facilitate and inform that influence.

There are many projects which can be undertaken; many more than a small college will have the resources to undertake. Again, selecting issues and questions that connect to the planning process can help to focus attention on research priorities (Uhl, 1983; Forter, 1983; Keller, 1983; Morrison et al, 1984). The following are some basic elements of a research program:

1. *What kind of students enroll in our college?*
   Have there been any changes in the pattern of enrollments in the last five years? By understanding the nature of the student body, admissions and retention issues can be anticipated. Changing interests, background, and educational experiences all have implications for student affairs and for college programs. If these data are not available, joint projects with the admissions office can be developed to provide this information including data about students who don't matriculate. Small colleges should explore the possibility of participation in national studies such as the Cooperative Institutional Research Program sponsored by ACE and UCLA and the Admissions Testing Program of the College Entrance Examination Board (CEEB). Such projects allow small colleges to obtain useful local and national information with minimal cost.

2. *How many students who matriculate go on to graduate and why?*
   Relatively few institutions have a good data base concerning retention. What is the graduation rate of entering freshmen, of transfers? What are the characteristics of those who leave compared to those who stay? What do freshmen, sophomores, juniors, and graduates think of the institution? What

are the institution's strengths and weaknesses from the student perspective? Scripps College has been involved in regular studies over the last ten years to understand the student experience at Scripps. Because of our size, we have been able to combine selective interviews with regular surveys of the student body. Interviews of the freshman class have been combined with surveys of the entire graduating class to become the cornerstone of Scripps data base on students. We also have conducted studies on those who withdraw to provide comparative data about those who stay and those who leave. Other institutions have built senior surveys into the research and planning program as well. Again, because of the size of small colleges, open-ended responses as well as readily quantifiable data can be integrated. Essay responses, for example, can be summarized, to allow selected administrators and faculty to read some of the verbatim responses (assuming respondents' anonymity can be protected).

3. *Alumni Profile*
Ideally, an institution will periodically survey alumni for information on strengths, weaknesses, satisfaction, and current position. This information has proven useful to admissions, to student affairs, and to academic programs (Kuh & Wallman, 1986).

These initiatives are clearly within the student affairs mission in a small college. There are other important questions not directly within the responsibility of student affairs that are also central to an institutional research program such as data on faculty, tenure ratios, and student/faculty ratios. By establishing the significance of research on students, and by demonstrating the connection between information on students and other aspects of the college, one can begin to develop collaborative arrangements with other programs to generate important, useful information.

Research with Limited Resources

Institutional research in the small college setting can be conducted with limited staff support. It is recommended that the research program, particularly in the early stages, be kept fairly simple and consistent over time so that changes can be studied.

It is more useful to develop a basic program of surveying seniors, or those who leave, that is analyzed regularly than to do a variety of "one time only" studies.

Every effort should be made to take advantage of the expertise often available either in the student affairs division or among the faculty. Faculty often find such research very useful and a matter of significant interest to them. Moreover, the process of involving others in the implementation of research increases the probability that the results will be used.

Another major resource for staffing can be provided by involving students through academic internships or work-study to assist in the design of research and, significantly, in the analysis of data. Such opportunities provide students with experience that may add to their own professional development. In the beginning of the Scripps institutional research effort, students made it possible to implement a research program. Each year one student was hired for ten hours a week to assist in the design of the research and to carry out the analysis of data. In recent years we have also involved students in writing articles to communicate the results of selected research back to the student body.

Another way to use resources effectively is to avoid asking, "Wouldn't it be interesting to know?" Often, even if we knew, we would not be able to make any use of the information. Ask first why it is important to know something and how results can be used. Similarly, avoid developing surveys from the very beginning. Nationally designed surveys or instruments from other institutions that can be modified can be very helpful.

Limited resources should be targeted to strengthen the connection between the ongoing planning and research process and the regular accreditation self-studies required of the institution. The self-study process requires data collection, but it can and should be organized around ongoing institutional issues and planning.

Increasing the Impact of the Program

Of fundamental importance in any effort of this sort is the effectiveness of the communication involved. If the research is to aid institutional planning, it must involve others.

1. Before finalizing surveys of analyses, ask other departments or offices if they have some issues or questions to ask which might be included in your study. Research is then seen as a joint venture. This is particularly important where sensitive areas of research are to be developed. By asking relevant constituencies such as faculty advisors or specific departments to assist in the design of research, the probability that the results will be used can be increased.

2. Do the analysis on the computer whenever possible. Since most institutions have access to some computers, the analysis can be done with much greater efficiency and ease. Moreover, computer analyses can be done in several different ways with little extra effort. One will often find that other members of the community will begin to ask student affairs personnel for the information broken down by departments or by home state of the student, or by sex, etc. Having dates entered on the computer with sufficient background information makes such additional analyses relatively easy. Even institutions without major computer resources can now make use of relatively inexpensive microcomputers for this purpose.

3. Analyze and interpret data with institutional questions in mind. Sending stacks of printouts to the president is not helpful. A brief, careful summary of data relevant to the issue being addressed will make any research of this sort much more useful.

4. Develop a spirit of collaboration whenever possible. New efforts at planning and research can appear to threaten the autonomy of constituencies and departments. One must be sensitive to questions that involve another constituency or department.

Conclusion

There is a great deal of debate in the literature about definitions of planning, the role of data, and the possibility of spending too much time on planning. However, little disagreement exists about the need for strategic planning based on accurate information about the institution and the external environment. For some colleges, planning will be a matter of survival; for others, it can mean the difference between excellence or mediocrity. Student affairs involvement in institutional research and planning can provide an opportunity and a model for the rest of the institution.

According to Cyert (1983), "We face a new situation in higher education. It holds some novel threats and presents some fresh opportunities. Given the uncertainty . . . college and university offices cannot allow their organizations to drift" (p. viii). A sound but simple approach to planning and research is feasible in the small college. It is also essential.

References

Bean, J. P., & Kuh, G. D. (1984). A typology of planning problems. *Journal of Higher Education, 55,* 35-55.

Chaffee, E. E. (1983). *Case studies in college strategy* Boulder, CO: National Center for Higher Education Management Systems.

Cope, R. F. (1981). *Strategic planning, management and decision making. AAHE-ERIC/Higher Education Research Report, No. 9,* Washington, D. C.: American Association for Higher Education.

Cyert, R. M. (1983). Foreword in Keller, G. *Academic strategy,* Baltimore: Johns Hopkins University Press, 1983.

Foster, M. (1983). Strategic planning: Reaching consensus about the future. *Journal of NAWDAC, 46*(3), 34-40.

Heydinger, R. B. (1980). Academic program planning in perspective. *New Directions for Institutional Research No. 28,* San Francisco: Jossey-Bass.

Keller, G. (1983). *Academic strategy: The management revolution in American higher education.* Baltimore: Johns Hopkins University Press.

Kerr, Clark. (1980). *Three thousand futures.* Carnegie Council on Policy Studies in Higher Education. San Francisco: Jossey-Bass.

Kuh, G. D., & Wallman, G. H. (1986). Outcomes-oriented marketing. In D. Hossler (Ed.), Managing collegiate enrollments. *New directions for higher education.* San Francisco: Jossey-Bass.

Morrison, J., Renfro, W. L., & Boncher, W. (1984). *Futures research and the strategic planning process: Implications for higher education.* ASHE-ERIC Research Report No. 9, Washington, D. C.

Peters, T. J., & Waterman, R. H., Jr. (1982). *In search of excellence,* New York: Harper & Row.

Peterson, P. M. Small independent colleges. *National Forum,* 65(3), 6-9.

Powers, D. R., & Powers, M. F. (1983). *Making participatory management work.* San Francisco: Jossey-Bass.

Smith, D. G. (1982). The next step beyond student development—becoming partners within our institutions. *NASPA Journal, 19*(4), 36-45.

Steiner, G., & Miner, J. B. (1977). *Management policy and strategy,* New York: Macmillan.

Uhl, N. (1983). *Using research for strategic planning. New directions for institutional research, No. 37.* San Francisco: Jossey-Bass.

Yavitz, B., & Newman, W. (1982). *Strategy in action.* New York: Free Press.

Chapter 4

Innovative Programming: The Small College Approach

Deborah L. Floyd, Wanda Hendricks, Steve Larson, Cheryl Mabey, Andrea C. McAleenan, Rebecca Mattson, Samuel Mazman, Roger Morris, and Raymond P. Rood

Human and financial resources are precious commodities at many small colleges. At times, the lack of resources can be an impetus for creative approaches to responding to identified needs. On other occasions, comprehensive plans to enhance the quality of student life result from self-studies, long-range planning exercises, or an impending crisis. Small colleges are continually required to be flexible in matching resources to needs.

Student development programming can be an integrating force within a small college community. To be effective, programming must respond to the reasons students matriculated to the college. What do students expect from the living environment? What difficulties are students encountering? What are students' aspirations and what can student affairs staff do to enable students to attain their goals?

Chapter Overview

In this chapter, eight examples of creative programming at small colleges are presented. While these examples are by no means exhaustive of the array of innovative programs across the country, they are illustrative of the kinds of activities being implemented in different settings to meet the needs of different student groups.

Orientation is an opportunity to provide new students with a clear statement of the mission and values of an institution and to make students aware of the possibilities inherent within the college community. Orientation also is a ceremonial affirmation of the student's decision to attend college and marks the initiation of a journey. The first creative programming description describes a comprehensive, continuous orientation program at Gordon College in Wenham, Massachusetts.

Many times colleges aspire to a comprehensive, holistic model of student development, but allow a fragmented system of programs and services to work against that process. The Life Planning Center model implemented at Scott Community College in Iowa is one innovative way to combine resources and provide more effective service delivery to students and is described in Section II.

Although most small colleges purport to train leaders for the future, many go about the process in a haphazard fashion. At Mount Saint Mary's College in Los Angeles, leadership development is a campus-wide concern. Efforts over a 10-year period have resulted in the establishment of a comprehensive student leadership program to which faculty, administration, and student affairs staff contribute resources, energy, and vision.

With the lack of broad resources for student programming and services, small colleges are always looking for ways to increase the quality of student life. In Section IV, a program at Whitman College in Washington integrates peer counseling in the career center with effective outreach efforts to community members and potential college donors. The synergy appears to benefit everyone.

West Shore Community College, located in a rural area of Michigan, developed a comprehensive computerized articulation process to streamline registration and advising. The program, described in Section V, makes use of innovations in technology, inter-institutional cooperation, and effective institutional teamwork on behalf of students.

One advantage small colleges may have compared with larger institutions is the higher level of coordination of developmental programming. For the environment to be developmentally powerful, this philosophy must be infused across a broad range of programs and services. One of the areas sometimes overlooked as growth-producing is discipline. Section VI describes a developmentally based discipline process at Gordon College in Massachusetts.

A healthy person functions at optimal levels in all areas of life. Student affairs staff place high priority on efforts to instill this vision in their students. At McKendree College in Illinois, a strategy has been developed for meeting this goal through a Wellness Program. Using the resources of the surrounding community, McKendree students take advantage of opportunities to examine various dimensions of personal growth through an array of seminars, dialogue, and hands-on participation.

Through courses, faculty-student relationships, and practical experiences such as assistantships and practica, graduate students begin to appreciate the kinds of development that can be nurtured in students. The final segment describes a graduate training program that seeks to instill in graduate students the value of personal and professional growth through the use of a comprehensive orals examination at Azusa Pacific University in California.

I. *Effective Orientation Programming Involves Everyone*

The preordinate goal in planning a small college orientation program is to ensure the support and involvement of the entire campus community, including faculty, staff, students, and especially academic administrators. Each area needs to understand the importance of orientation and provide the necessary support through personal involvement and contribution of resources. The spirit of unity and cooperation established during these few days goes a long way in developing a sense of spirit and unity for the entire year by creating a cooperative partnership between all areas on campus. Orientation can provide an introduction to the culture and character of the campus, the first step in teaching new students about the institution's saga. In turn, the retention rate and degree of satisfaction on the part of students and parents are enhanced.

Gordon College, a small residential campus of 1,200 students in northeastern Massachusetts, has a campus-wide orientation program that encourages cooperative planning through mutual accountability which reinforces the principle that "we're on the same team." All of the college's administrators are involved to some degree in planning and implementing the program. Table 1 depicts the campus personnel involved in various aspects of the orientation process.

Greek Night is the opening orientation evening event sponsored jointly by the admissions and orientation offices. During this event, small groups are formed that meet throughout the fall term with an upper class peer leader. The admission staff has the opportunity to solicit prospective student names through an innovative game which gives the admission staff a significant role in the transition from pre-school to on-campus activities. The *Campus Hunt* is a scavenger hunt where new students become acquainted with the college's facilities and also meet key campus personnel. The *Variety Show* is an all-campus event featuring faculty, staff, and students performing dance, music, and comedy acts. The night before academic advising and registration, *faculty desserts* are hosted by faculty members in their homes for new students planning to major in the faculty member's field.

For orientation to be effective, a committed but representative group of students must be involved in facilitating the program. At Gordon, approximately 40 students work with the director to design and implement the annual program. They begin with a comprehensive training program during the spring term prior to orientation and continue with weekly meetings during the fall to plan for their leadership role in the Freshman Convocation program.

One way to increase retention is to view orientation as a "continuing" experience (Dannells & Kuh, 1977). Initial efforts

Table 1

EFFECTIVE PROGRAM PLANNING FOR THE SMALL COLLEGE:

CREATING A CAMPUS-WIDE ORIENTATION MODEL

Gordon College
Wenham, Massachusetts

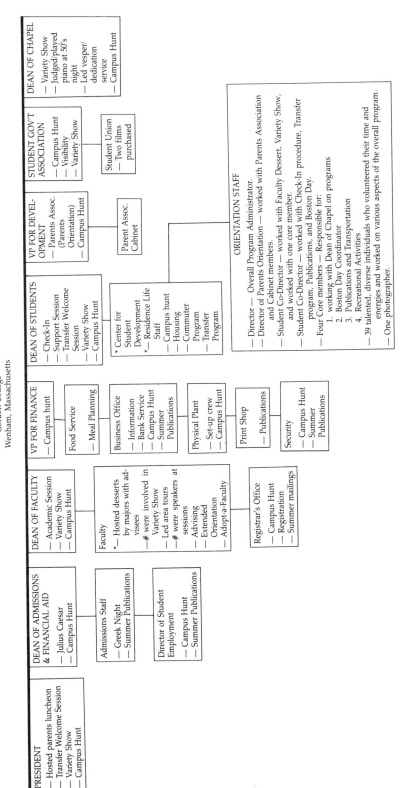

to institutionalize an extended orientation program occurred at Gordon College in 1983 with the establishment of a Freshman Convocation. During orientation, each new freshman becomes part of a group that continues to meet throughout the fall term as part of weekly convocation. Upper class student leaders (orientation staff) are joined by a faculty member and a Center for Student Development staff member committed to: (1) introducing the students to the meaning and potential of personal growth in the collegiate environment; and (2) describing the resources available throughout the college to assist with the process. Assessments of personal interests, competencies, and values are made to help students to begin to establish goals and to document progress throughout the year.

A second phase of the extended orientation program focuses on a select group of new students with extraordinary potential, the A.J. Gordon Scholars. These students meet individually and as a group with a mentor assigned from the student development staff for the purposes of: (1) assessing personal strengths and interests; (2) establishing short- and long-range goals; (3) monitoring progress toward goals; (4) encouraging participation in various leadership experiences on campus; (5) initiating the development of a personal portfolio; and (6) introducing the learner's journal for the purpose of processing insights about life.

The Orientation and Freshman Convocation programs are in the third year of operation and have been systematically evaluated and refined based on recommendations from participants. Student comments are generally positive and suggest that the program allays some fears about college and assists with the development of a framework for the intentional pursuit of academic and personal goals.

II. *Life Planning Center: A Holistic Approach to Student Development in a Small Community College Setting*

The first question students are frequently asked is, "What is your major?" Unfortunately, students often select areas of study without adequate interest and ability assessments, specific information about various career fields, and realistic life goals. While most student affairs professionals recognize the value of career planning, systematic efforts in career evaluation usually occur after the admissions process is complete and the student is enrolled for classes. In 1985, Scott Community College created a Life Planning Center to systematically assist students in career and life planning from admission through graduation.

The 2,800 credit students who enroll at Scott Community College (SCC) each term have two major goals. Those in transfer fields aspire to complete courses and transfer with junior status to a senior college. Students in the vocational-technical fields aspire to learn skills in two years or less that will lead to a good job. As with most community colleges, SCC students are heterogeneous in terms of age, academic abilities, socioeconomic background, and aspirations. Since the students represent diverse developmental backgrounds and do not enjoy the benefits of a residential environment, the obstacles they must overcome to realize their goals are great indeed.

SCC staff worked for several years to develop systems and programs to help various types of students achieve success. By 1985, many key support systems were in place; however, one major challenge remained: providing personalized attention for students' academic and career aspirations. Students with questions about admission went to one office, for counseling they made an appointment with staff from another office, and for financial aid information yet another office was involved. New students rarely visited the job placement office as a part of making initial career decisions. Due to the fact most students leave within two years or less, it was decided that a centralized, "one stop shopping" approach was needed from the point of admission through exit.

The Life Planning Center was designed to integrate the functions of admissions, academic advising, career planning, referral to various agencies and services, transfer articulation, and job placement. The major charge of the new Life Planning Center was to holistically facilitate students' life and career planning from admission through completion of the SCC experience.

"While 'life planning' is not a new term, in divisions of student affairs the Life Planning Center is an emerging alternative organizational approach. It is based on the student development philosophy that the intentional development of its clients, regardless of background is paramount" (Adams, 1980, pp. 225-26). Most of the LPC models described by Adams included a career resource center, experiential programs, counseling support, courses and seminars, and assessment center and job placement. The SCC Life Planning Center is unique from other known LPC models in that the office of admissions plays a critical role. By including the admissions function, students are able to begin their career and life planning from the point of their initial contact with the college. Admissions processes have become more than simply filling out forms, since students have an opportunity to explore career fields, participate in ability and interest assessments, learn about senior colleges and universities, and explore job leads and market analysis information — all in the same room with staff who become familiar with their range of needs and aspirations.

Concurrent with the opening of the Life Planning Center, the existing counseling staff were decentralized and reassigned to academic divisions. Counselors were charged with responsibilities that required more interaction with faculty and increased contacts with students about academic issues. A counseling referral system was established to include systematic procedures for referrals from LPC staff to counselors on a regular basis. Counselors generally refer students to the LPC for career resource exploration, computerized guidance experiences, and job and transfer information. Although full-time counselors are not housed in the Life Planning Center, they assume regular "lab hours" to assist with drop-ins, to ensure open communication with LPC staff, and to maintain an efficient referral system.

Lack of resources was one of the most common reasons given by chief student affairs administrators in small community colleges for not implementing innovative student development programs (Floyd, 1980). The Life Planning Center was created with existing staff resources. Through organizational and physical plant cooperation, the functions of admissions, academic and career guidance support, and job placement/articulation assistance, were centralized under one organization. Staff began to work more closely as a team to implement valued student development goals. Cross training of staff and other aspects of job sharing has become the norm in the LPC. Staffed with paraprofessional, clerical, administrative, and peer advising personnel, the LPC staff plan and implement programs and activities to encourage students to achieve worthwhile life and career goals.

Although the Life Planning Center is still relatively new, initial reactions of students and staff have been positive. Students seem to benefit from this personalized, holistic approach afforded by centralizing admissions, advising, career resources, and job placement/transfer support in the same office suite. The need for students to move from office to office for assistance has been dramatically reduced, and faculty have expressed their satisfaction in having counselors available in their academic setting for day-to-day consultation.

Effective life planning and the realization of student success is a significant challenge which requires a substantial commitment. The implementation of a new Life Planning Center has reaffirmed to students and others that Scott Community College is committed to students' development. As the LPC evolves, plans include providing specialized support for adults reentering college, increasing the number of seminars and courses offered, improving transfer articulation process, enhancing job placement successes, and increasing the involvement of faculty in student life-planning processes.

III. *The Student Development Professional: A Catalyst for Leadership Development in a Small College*

Among the many challenges facing educators is the responsibility to foster effective citizenship and to educate leaders of society. Some colleges explicitly intend to develop students' leadership capabilities. Educational practice seldom approximates rhetorical intentions, however. Researchers suggest that colleges are doing little to promote leadership development among their students; instead they merely are giving some students the means to exhibit existing abilities. Student affairs staff are pivotal to successfully meeting the challenge to educate for leadership.

Assumptions

Leadership research is scattered throughout the literature of various disciplines including political science, history, philosophy, psychology, business management, organizational theory, and speech communication. Since leadership theory extends beyond traditional disciplines, the study of leadership studies typically does not have a central place in the curriculum. The first step in implementing an institutional approach to leadership is to encourage an interdisciplinary approach to the academic study of leadership, or to make courses on leadership available through appropriate departments. Leadership studies provide a means for student affairs staff to interact with faculty in a meaningful, non-territorial fashion.

The second assumption is that leadership training involves a cognitive dimension, in that students must understand definitions, theory, and styles of leadership, and it must provide an opportunity for students to internalize and use leadership skills. Leadership involves KNOWING and DOING. A college must encourage students to experience the nexus between theory and practice that functionally requires cooperation — a joint venture — between the academic community and student affairs.

A third assumption is quantitative. A certain percentage of students currently enrolled must be involved in leadership studies or leadership development programs. Limiting the development of leadership skills to elected student leaders is not sufficient to merit an institutional approach. The college must provide opportunities for students to apply their leadership skills and to discuss what the ends of leadership are. Not only do the opportunities need to be diverse and encompass student activities, community service, and professional opportunities, but leadership experiences also must permit students access to the locus of power at the institution. Whether the power resides in faculty committees, at the presidential staff or cabinet level, with the trustees or regents, or in some combination, an institutional commitment to leadership development requires that decision-making opportunities be available. Student affairs staff can identify students who would benefit from leadership training and can also lobby for expanded opportunities for student membership within the college.

Finally, evaluative measures are needed to assess to what extent the college is meeting the leadership development objective. Since leadership itself is complex, any evaluation needs to be multivariate. Longitudinal data are necessary to infer the benefits of leadership training for college students. Specific inventories which measure a student's understanding of leadership theories coupled with self-assessments should be administered systematically. Most important, the information gathered should be regularly disseminated to administrators and faculty. Once again, student affairs staff can be the catalyst for such evaluations.

Mount St. Mary's College Leadership Program

Mount St. Mary's College is the only Catholic women's college in the western United States. The college has a long history of commitment to leadership development for women. This is stated explicitly in the mission statement of the college. In 1974-75 the college received an unrestricted private gift that was dedicated to scholarships for graduating high school students "with leadership potential." Within five years, the program was available to any Mount student interested in leadership. The four-year program grew from 13 students to over 250 students.

Additional corporate, foundation, and governmental funding furthered the efforts of the college to provide leadership training for women. The Budget Committee and Resource Development staff now have the means to ensure the success of the campus-wide efforts. In fact, funds have been obtained to establish a Leadership Center to facilitate training of high school students in southern California. The Center, staffed by leadership students at the college, is now generating revenue for its services.

Pre- and post-test evaluations of the program demonstrate that students modify their assumptions about group behavior and effective leadership within six months, while their peers do not. Leadership students have developed the ability to analyze different leadership theories, master specific leadership skills, alter leadership styles, and identify areas in which they intend to emerge as leaders. Leadership students report a significant increase in self-confidence, involvement in public policy issues, interest in graduate education, and non-traditional careers for women to a much larger extent than do non-leadership students. Furthermore, the college retention rate of leadership students is twice as high as that of students not in the program.

Data about the impact of the program are gathered by student affairs staff within six months after the students enter the college and continue to be collected, including an assessment of outcomes prior to graduation. Alumnae surveys assess attitudes and outcomes one year, five years, and ten years after graduation. Ten years of research indicate that when an institution-wide approach exists, leadership development flourishes.

The basic components of this leadership effort consist of:

1. A core curriculum in leadership open to all entering students taught by student affairs staff

2. Expanded co-curricular involvement and leadership training opportunities to improve students' leadership skills which are supervised by student affairs staff

3. Garnering institution-wide support for the curricular and co-curricular efforts in leadership development through the initiative of the student affairs staff.

Curriculum Offerings

The core curriculum of the leadership program open to all entering students includes at least three one-unit seminars:

a. Introduction to leadership theories and style

b. Leadership skill-building related to productivity and communication

c. Advanced leadership focused upon case studies involving motivation, change, and leadership situations.

Student affairs staff have developed and taught all three courses. The academic background of these staff members, which includes both the humanities and social sciences, is well known and respected by the faculty.

In addition to the leadership curriculum core, courses are available in public speaking, career planning, introduction to peer counseling, and departmental internships. The staff are actively involved in each of these offerings either as instructors or consultants to departments.

Co-Curriculum Involvement/Leadership Training Opportunities

There has been a great increase in student involvement since the college has emphasized the learning opportunities available through student activities. Over the past 10 years, the number of students from each entering class active in a peer counseling or student government position has increased from 20% to over 60%. Student affairs staff view student activities as a laboratory to practice leadership skills. Members of the staff explicitly recommend that students plan and select one peer counseling experience to improve communication or helping skills, and at least one governance experience to gain experience with task-oriented, productive work groups. Through freshman interviews conducted by student affairs professionals and annual student activities inventories, students' involvement is encouraged and monitored.

Other examples of leadership training opportunities include: (1) an annual orientation session open to all student leaders during the summer; (2) a student advocacy class open to all student leaders taught for credit throughout the year; (3) a midyear assessment workshop available upon request for any student organization; (4) an annual leadership conference which attracts over 100 students for an intensive weekend of personal and leadership development; and (5) the opportunity to facilitate high school leadership training as part of the Leadership Center.

Institutional Involvement in Leadership Development

The student affairs staff has enjoyed positive, active support of the college president in institutionalizing the college's approach to leadership development. The student affairs staff's successful integration of leadership efforts with the institutional mission has been crucial for garnering broad-based support for the curricular and co-curricular efforts in leadership development. Through the active involvement of student affairs staff in preparation of annual reports, faculty forums, student moderators' mini-workshops, and various task forces and committees on curriculum development, a sense of collaboration has been fostered throughout the college. The Leadership Program is not owned by the Student Development staff, although organizationally it is assigned to student affairs.

Examples of the institution-wide involvement in leadership development opportunities for students and staff include: faculty forums analyzing faculty leadership styles, faculty members requesting sabbaticals in leadership studies, two departmental curriculum revisions to include the leadership program, one department requiring leadership courses of its majors, and faculty participation and attendance in leadership seminars. Likewise, administrative decisions concerning student policies have been made with consideration for the learning environment necessary to foster leadership. Residential policies in particular have been reviewed and changed to shift more responsibility to the students.

Summary

A small college can experiment in systematizing and broadening education for leadership in a way that a larger, state-funded university may find difficult. For example, a small college usually has less "red tape," a faster decision-making process, and fewer actors involved. Student affairs staff can meet regularly with faculty members, have access to important committees, and disseminate working papers and research results college-wide.

A small college provides a context in which to experiment with education for leadership on an institutional basis. The case study of the past 10 years at Mount St. Mary's College suggests that an important mission can be explicitly operationalized through an active student affairs staff, presidential support, faculty involvement, collaboration among staffs, and the use of public and private funds.

IV. *Students as Paraprofessionals*

Peers have a strong influence on one another. Student parapro-fessionals have the potential to accomplish certain program goals more effectively than student affairs staff or faculty. Para-professional programs offer a forum for the development of stu-dent leadership and growth. A by-product is that they can often serve as an excellent marketing tool for the college. Effective student leadership development programs impress prospective students and their parents, alumni, potential employers, and donors (Kuh & Wallman, 1986). Paraprofessionals also enrich the lives of the professionals with whom they work.

Whitman College, founded in 1859, is an independent liber-al arts institution with 1,100 students, 90% of whom live on cam-pus. Whitman is a traditional, highly academic college in the New England tradition. In keeping with the college's interest in extending its educational program throughout the community, the Career Center's paraprofessional program now provides students with the opportunity to develop and expand their growth and autonomy in a learning environment outside the classroom. Paraprofessionals are trained to plan, execute, and implement seven major programs: recruitment, internships, ex-ternships, workshops, summer jobs, the career library, and communications. Each student develops and maintains a specif-ic program, selects and manages a committee, sets goals, moni-tors progress, and markets the program to the Whitman com-munity.

Paraprofessionals have also been involved in: (1) teaching students in résumé writing and interviewing workshops; (2) conducting personal visits to companies to encourage them to recruit on campus; (3) giving presentations about the program to professional conferences, alumni and parent groups; (4) writing and producing major office publications; (5) developing guide-books on interviewing and internships; and (6) serving as hosts for campus visitors.

The students meet weekly with a professional staff member to set goals and evaluate the previous week's work. Focusing on the difficulties and rewards faced by the peer manager, the pro-fessional offers reactions and suggestions in the form of affirmation and challenge, and assesses the need for further training. Paraprofessionals also participate in weekly staff meetings with professional staff to discuss items related to in-service training and student concerns.

One of the most creative programs initiated at the Center is "Student Futures." Paraprofessionals began speaking at alumni gatherings to explain how alumni could be involved in preparing students for a successful life after college. In turn the entire campus community benefited from the linkages between student paraprofessionals and the alumni who experienced an on-going connection to the campus through the outreach program.

The growth and development of paraprofessional staff members has been assessed through interviews, self-reports, and observations by professional staff. Participants have exhibited growth in the areas of autonomy, competence, and interdependence. They have gained valuable experience in working with professionals and peers while acquiring an understanding and appreciation for student development theory. Each student is also responsible for selecting and training a successor. The students demonstrate a high personal investment in the goals of the Center and generate energy and activity for all of the programs.

The use of students as paraprofessionals offers a creative and effective solution to the small college's age-old problem of limited financial and human resources and provides a challenging learning experience consistent with the goals of higher education. A commitment to a dynamic paraprofessional program places student affairs in an influential leadership role that can favorably impact the college and its constituents.

V. A Different Approach to an Old Problem: Computerized Articulation of Transfer Credits

Students who lose credit or receive "general elective" credit for courses they expected would satisfy specific requirements at four-year institutions are quick to communicate their disappointment to friends who may be considering a community college for the first two years of an undergraduate degree. Indeed, transfer programs at community colleges usually are considered credible if community college courses are granted credit by a receiving senior institution. Articulation programs and agreements between institutions have become more numerous and problem free as both community colleges and four-year institutions recognize that a smooth transition benefits both. Communicating the details of these programs in a timely way to students then becomes critical to the transfer process.

Many community colleges do not require students to participate in counseling or academic advising sessions. In fact, colleges with on-line phone registration programs may allow students to enroll in courses without ever coming to the campus. Students residing in distant rural areas or who wish to avoid traffic congestion are spared the commitment of time and money to register, solving one problem. However convenient, this may create another problem: many students wish to enroll in courses that are not directly relevant to students' ultimate goals. Without personal advising, small colleges may miss the opportunity to help students design an appropriate program of study.

At West Shore Community College (WSCC) in Scottsville, Michigan, an attempt to remedy this situation took the form of a transfer process that integrated articulation data, the master student record, and fee statements. The first step was to build a crosswalk (matrix) of course transfer equivalencies for each of the senior institutions to which most of the WSCC students transferred. All but a small percentage of students transferred to one of eight Michigan schools. Thus, eight banks of crosswalk data were created in the computer system. The second step was to provide a linkage between the crosswalks and the registration process. Each senior institution was assigned a code number, and the registration program was expanded to allow the input of one of these codes as identified by the students. This code served as an important identification point for each student's proposed schedule.

Finally, the statement of fees included a schedule of classes for which the student was enrolled, and became a suitable vehicle through which to communicate course evaluation decisions such as: (1) All courses transfer to [institution]; (2) * = This course does not transfer to . . . ; (3) # = This course transfers with restriction to . . .; and (4) All other courses transfer to. . . . Message 1 indicates an appropriate selection of courses for the intended transfer institution. If a course on the schedule is flagged with an asterisk, Message 2 appears on the fee statement, pointing out problems. In the event a course is flagged with a #, the student knows that that course transfers for certain majors only. Message 4 may accompany Messages 2 and/or 3 as appropriate.

There are additional capabilities built into the program. If after one or more semesters a student wants to transfer to a different institution than originally indicated, the entire transcript can be reproduced against any of the crosswalks to determine what the effect will be. Academic advisors are especially appreciative of this feature, as it is no longer necessary to spend considerable time referencing hard copy articulation documents. In addition, a copy of the transfer equivalency is routinely attached to each official academic transcript sent to an educational institution. Once WSCC demonstrates the verisimilitude of transcripts to admissions counselors and credentials analysts at other institutions, the time required to evaluate WSCC transcripts is considerably diminished. If discrepancies are noted during articulation, the WSCC staff enters into a dialogue with the receiving institution on behalf of the student.

Since the WSCC system is on-line and resolves a major concern for accuracy, it has received considerable attention from other institutions and has become a useful marketing and recruitment tool. Another unexpected benefit was realized shortly after implementation. Senior institution admissions officers have used the WSCC comprehensive college printout to persuade division chairs to recognize WSCC courses for credit when they may have been reluctant to do so previously. When admissions officers demonstrate that a large percentage of sister institutions are recognizing particular course(s), there is less resistance to follow the trend.

In the past two years, substantial growth has been noted in the reverse transfer population at WSCC; e.g., students who started at or attended a senior institution and are transferring to the community college. The time spent evaluating transcripts is considerably reduced as staff need only to input the courses and the computer produces WSCC equivalent courses. While this process may appear quite routinized, it does illustrate how a small college can design a system to efficiently respond to the needs of a diverse student body. Innovative programming can relate pragmatically to personal long-term academic and career needs, thereby increasing the positive impact a small community college can have on its constituencies.

VI. *Discipline Viewed in Developmental Terms*

Institutional policies and procedures are implemented by student affairs staff members based on a collective understanding of the character and mission of the college. At Gordon College in Wenham, Massachusetts, the discipline process emphasizes personal accountability or self-discipline. Developmental theory suggests that as students mature into adulthood, they begin to become less dependent on externally imposed rules to govern behavior and better able to discern what is right, independent of peer and familial expectations. This process occurs at different rates and is manifested in various ways. Sometimes students' behavior exceeds acceptable parameters defined by the college. In such instances, college authorities — peer counselors, residence hall directors, judiciary boards, or deans — often become involved.

The discipline process at Gordon attempts to understand the root cause(s) of misbehavior and to respond with justice and mercy, as opposed to a superficial analysis of the situation and a "law and order" response. The college seeks to maintain a balance between love and justice. The goals of the discipline process are to encourage personal responsibility and to avoid sanctions that are either overly hard or overly soft.

Encouraging self-responsibility and integrity is initiated by a presidential address at orientation, during which the college's expectations for behavior are outlined. Follow-up sessions with the orientation and residential life staff reinforce these expectations and involve students in ongoing discussions held during the subsequent orientation classes.

Students are expected to maintain standards consistent with a Christian world view. Given the atmosphere of free inquiry on liberal arts campuses, it is not surprising that the legitimacy of certain standards are annually discussed and debated. Nonetheless, the demands of community life require mutual understandings; Gordon College's position is that neither the difficulty of the task nor the inevitable imperfections should keep the college community from maintaining reasonable expectations for all members. Understanding what it means to join a community dedicated to fostering learning in the intellectual, spiritual, personal, and physical domains requires that students confront values, opinions, and ideas that may be different and new. Through this process students encounter opportunities to stretch and grow, to test attitudes, and to learn how to live in a communal setting, to explore the broad range of human opinion and ideas without necessarily engaging in the whole range of human behavior.

The Gordon approach has been to give the student the freedom, without becoming antinomian, to consciously develop responsibility without becoming legalistic. By engaging the student in dialogue about the meaning of self-discipline, responsibility and integrity, the student is both supported and challenged in efforts to develop congruent values. Many students are encouraged to develop specific growth contracts for which they will be held accountable. These contracts are developed by the student with support from a student development staff member. The main focus is on the area of difficulty; however, often staff are able to use this opportunity to encourage students to examine broader goals affecting other areas of life.

Every college approaches discipline in some ways that may be similar. The Gordon College example is not presented as the single best or "right" approach. Instead, it is offered as an illustration of how one college strives to make discipline policies and procedures congruent with its mission.

VII. *Programming Wellness for the Total Person*

Successful wellness programs created and implemented at small colleges have four essential components: (1) a programming philosophy; (2) little or no cost; (3) involvement of the entire college community; and (4) creative staff to tap the resources within the nearby community, including higher education institutions and professional colleagues. At McKendree College, a small liberal arts college (FTE 400) in Lebanon, Illinois, these elements were combined to create a Wellness Model based on a developmental approach.

For students to make enlightened choices about their education and life, individuals need to inventory individual abilities, capabilities, limitations, and goals. The purpose of a comprehensive wellness model is to encourage growth in various domains: intellectual, emotional, physical, social, vocational, and spiritual. This broad range of goals enabled McKendree College to look far beyond the academic dimensions of a student's life and embrace a more holistic view of development.

Based on several of the growth components developed by Hernandez, Kestutis, Phillips, and Woodly (cited in Woniak, 1983), McKendree College designed a wellness model that encompasses six dimensions of growth:

1. *Intellectual Development* — Encourages creative, stimulating mental activities in and out of the classroom. Student programming ideas:

> a. Scholastic Bowl, a program designed to stimulate intellectual competition outside the classroom, was coordinated by students and faculty. Faculty members provided academic questions, served as judges, timekeepers, and moderators. Teams were composed of student clubs and organizations;

> b. Male/Female Relationships program used the Meyers-Briggs Type Inventory to explore expectations in relationships, personality types, and how they affect relationships;

> c. "The Last Lecture of Your Life Series" was designed to give faculty, staff, and students an opportunity to lecture on topics important to them.

2. *Emotional Development* — Encourages awareness and acceptance of one's feelings by increasing positive feelings about oneself and life. Student programming ideas:

    a. Test Anxiety — Desensitization sessions that are particularly helpful to first-year students in decreasing anxiety;

    b. Stress-reduction programs that incorporate techniques used in text anxiety workshops to minimize stress in all facets of student's life;

    c. An eight-week Assertiveness Training Seminar offered to students, staff, and faculty.

3. *Physical Development* — Encourages assessment of knowledge about food and nutrition, discourages substance abuse, and promotes cardiovascular, flexibility, and body improvement activities. Student programming ideas:

    a. Aerobics classes, lap swimming, running, water polo, volleyball games, and pickle ball;

    b. Alcohol Awareness programs sponsored during National Alcohol Awareness Week was a campuswide event;

    c. Nutrition information sessions are beneficial to those who desire weight reduction.

4. *Social Development* — Encourages contributions to the human and physical welfare of the community through fostering interdependence with others and nature, and understanding territoriality, shared space, and personal differentiation concepts. Student programming ideas:

    a. Faculty/Staff Follies and New Game, the Roommate Game, and Floor Feud;

    b. Food drives for the needy;

    c. Blood drives for the American Red Cross;

d. Handicapable Awareness Days/Week consisted of assuming a physical disability, i.e., blindness, deafness, or being a paraplegic for a day;

e. Room personalization by allowing students to build lofts in rooms if the room furniture is not built in;

f. Floor mural personalization competition;

g. On the 50th anniversary of residence halls, students were given flowers and tree seedlings to plant around campus.

5. *Vocational Development* — Encourages preparation for work in which one will gain personal satisfaction and enrichment through self-assessment and career exploration. Student programming ideas:

a. College fairs, invitations to corporations, nonprofit agencies, and businesses, to provide information about employment opportunities;

b. Women's Awareness Month — women in nontraditional positions, i.e., plumbers, electricians, morticians, bankers, a judge, and a financial planner were invited to speak as panel members focusing on the theme, "Carving New Careers."

6. *Spiritual Development* — Encourages students to seek for the meaning and purpose of human existence. Student programming ideas:

a. Films, speakers (faculty or international students) and slide shows about various religions;

b. Ethnic dinners with Chinese decorations and the College Troupe performing Chinese dances.

Through the use of the campus-wide Wellness Model, McKendree students are exposed to significant issues of holistic development at minimal cost. The interaction, dialogue, shared resources, and involvement of students, staff, and others increase the chances that students will benefit from the small college experience.

VIII. *The Small College Perspective in Graduate Training*

Most of the student affairs staff members working in small colleges have graduate degrees from large universities. Graduates of the masters level program in Student Development at Azusa Pacific University in Azusa, California are exceptions. This institution of 1,500 on-campus students offers liberal arts and professional programs at both the undergraduate and masters degree level. In 1973, a graduate preparation program was initiated at Azusa Pacific to prepare specialists in small college administration. Although the program has expanded to embrace human resource development, the application of human development theory in small college settings has endured as a basic component of the two-year student affairs graduate preparation program.

Each student participates in a variety of experiential opportunities in diverse programmatic settings designed to assist them in developing a generalist perspective in addition to refining a specialized area of competence (e.g., career planning, financial aids, student ministries, residence life). Opportunities for exposure to various aspects of the field come in the form of internships, practica, and on the job experiences. Since many student affairs professionals at small colleges must assume considerable responsibility at a relatively young age, laboratories that offer supervised experiences are critical. An important aspect of the Azusa program is student involvement with campuswide task forces, faculty committees, lectures in various classes, and assistance with off-campus programming. Each of these opportunities reinforces one of the distinctive features of small colleges — the opportunity to interact with faculty and staff on campus-wide initiatives and programs.

One of the most innovative aspects of this small college program is the Graduate Oral Examination. The purpose of the oral exam is to give each student an opportunity to translate developmental theory into practice and to describe to peers, students, faculty, and administrators how theory can be used. The exam requires each student to articulate a philosophy of student development - to be certain it is fully integrated and personally owned. The process helps students focus on what was particularly significant during the program. The question of what affected one's life (both positively and negatively) is dealt with in depth.

Following a written comprehensive examination, an oral defense is scheduled in March of the second year of the program to allow ample time for processing the experience and to follow through on any issues needing further exploration prior to graduation. The orals portion of the examination assists students in translating the entire graduate experience into a systematic job search plan. Since the completion of the graduate program marks a significant professional and personal transition, the orals provide a ritual of celebration of this achievement. Each student prepares for the exam both in written and oral fashion. Each student presents the summary to the people who have been most involved in their journey during the past two years. Participants include the director of the graduate program, the internship supervisor or professional position supervisor, a faculty member, a peer from the graduate program, and a fifth participant who can be anyone (spouse, friend, parent, mentor). Invitations are also sent out by the student to anyone else he or she wishes to attend. (This varies between 5-50.)

The format varies also. For example, one student chose to describe her experience through a multi-media presentation complete with live dance and personally composed music; another demonstrated her journey through painting and sketches completed during the program and contrasting them with her art prior to entering the program.

The intensity of the graduate program with its close, powerful community context requires a period of closure prior to a new beginning. The orals provide this opportunity. After the presentation, students are given feedback on their areas of strength and other areas that need to be explored or developed further. In follow up sessions, the student works with participants to determine how the information gleaned can become part of a continuing growth experience that facilitates, not debilitates.

While this strategy is both time consuming and energy draining, the results have been remarkable. Students believe they are far better prepared to enter the field after this process of synthesis and declaration. It is also illustrative of the type of individualized programming possible in small college environments. It enables professionals new to student affairs work to become thoroughly versed in the types of growth processes they can, in turn, inspire in the students with whom they will work.

Postscript

These eight examples underscore the broad range of student affairs programming initiatives that address students' developmental needs. While the entire scope of creative programming possibilities are far too numerous to treat in a single chapter, these illustrative programs are meant to stimulate dialogue and action on the part of small college student affairs staff and students. Other topics such as decision making, time management, depression, sexual identity, life planning skills, and the use and misuse of alcohol also require attention if the developmental aims of the academy are to be furthered.

Programming for student development calls for creativity, flexibility, and an ability to respond sensitively and holistically to students. The potential is enormous, the challenges clear.

References

Adams, D. T. (1980). Life planning centers. In F. B. Newton K. L. & Ender (Eds.), *Student development practices: Strategies for making a difference.* (pp. 225-243). Springfield, Illinois: Thomas.

Dannells, M., & Kuh, G. D. (1977). Orientation. In W. T. Packwood (Ed.), *College student personnel services* (pp. 102-124). Springfield, Illinois: Thomas.

Floyd, D. L. (1980). Chief student personnel administrators in small, rural, community colleges: A profile. *Southern College Personnel Association Journal, 3*(1), 25-34.

Kuh, G. D., & Wallman, G. H. (1986). Outcomes oriented marketing. In D. Hossler (Ed.), Managing collegiate enrollments. *New Directions for Higher Education.* San Francisco: Jossey-Bass.

Woniak, D. (1983). *Wellness programming manual.* Macomb, Illinois: Western Illinois University.

Chapter 5

Notes on Student Affairs Administration in the Small College

Robert B. Young

The basic premise of this chapter is that small college administration differs from large university administration. That assertion is difficult to prove, since small colleges take many forms. As McAleenan and Kuh mentioned in Chapter One, small colleges differ in size, locale, control, and curriculum, just like their larger counterparts. Although the "typical" small college does not exist, there is a collective identity, or ideology, that distinguishes the small college from a large multiversity (Young, 1986).

The small college ideology is characterized by synergy, values education, personalized relationships, and organic change. Conversely, the ideology of a large institution includes specialization, service and research, quantification, and rapid adaptation to the needs of society (Young, 1986). The small college ideology supports judgments that the small college differs from a large college in the quality of education, which is a function of qualitatively different, more intense patterns of human relationships. Some of the ideological characteristics of small and large institutions reflect differences in the type of control (public vs.

private) and curriculum as well as size. More important, the ideological differences between large and small institutions debunk the notions that small colleges are simply miniature versions of larger institutions and that student affairs administration in small colleges is simply "smaller" in scale than its counterpart in larger colleges. Small college student affairs work differs in some fundamental ways. Consider the following unique opportunities for staff in small colleges.

Young staff members can try different jobs in student affairs and in other divisions of the college. They can compete for the same leadership positions as in larger institutions, but against fewer candidates. They can administer projects which don't usually include student affairs administrators in larger institutions (e.g., institutional advancement). They can become personally acquainted with all of the people (faculty and students) in all of the programs at an institution.

In this chapter, small college student affairs administration is discussed in the context of two characteristics of the small college ideology, synergy and personalism. Then three additional role functions of small college student affairs staff (counseling, instruction, and consultation), are described. The chapter concludes with some professional development advantages of student affairs work in small colleges.

Synergy and Personalism

Synergy and personalism, two of the guiding values of the small college, have been emphasized in the student affairs literature for many years. Wrenn (1967) proposed that the evolution of student affairs as a field of practice required integration in the structure of institutions of higher education (synergy) and efforts to offset the quantification of students (personalism). Brown (1972) suggested some essential elements of a preferred set of student affairs functions, including a campus-wide appreciation of The Student Personnel Point of View (synergy), direct curricular involvement, and some type of direct contact with every student (personalism). Synergy helps to explain why administrators are involved with counseling, consultation, and instruction in student affairs programs in small colleges. Personalism means that meaningful relationships between and among students and staff are vital in small colleges. Encouraging high quality interpersonal relationships is a high priority for small college student affairs staff.

While specialization is valued in larger institutions, the integration of multiple roles, synergy, is important in small colleges. Multiple job functions and diverse duties are more characteristic of small college administrators than of university administrators (Floyd, 1980). But multiple responsibilities are not synergetic by themselves. They can drain administrators if they are not adequately blended together. The synergetic principle of student affairs practice in small colleges is student growth through contact with students. That principle can also be called "personalism," a term that emphasizes the importance of the individual as the basic unit of value in the small college (*Academic American Encyclopedia*, 1980).

According to Astin (1984), the degree of student development during college is directly proportional to the quality and quantity of student involvement with people and programs there. Riesman (1981) contended that small colleges are beneficial for many students because they offer security and involvement for those who need it. Because of the size of the institution, the student affairs administrator can become personally acquainted with most students. Unlike larger institutions, staff-student relationships are not limited to a few leaders or misanthropes. Any administrator, including the CSAO, can personally affect the development of a large portion of the undergraduate population. In many large universities, student affairs administrators move from primary responsibilities for student counseling as entry level staff to management responsibilities as senior administrators. Student contact diminishes as managerial responsibilities increase in large colleges and universities. But student contact remains important throughout the careers of all small college administrators, even as staff supervision increases. Vice presidents of student affairs have more contacts with students than with any other constituency on campus (Astin & Scherrei, 1980). In a 1982 NASPA small college survey, mid-level and chief administrators reported that "seeing growth" in individual students brought them the greatest satisfaction in their careers (Byrne & Rooney, 1983). These findings are supported by the contributors to Chapters Six and Seven.

Personalism is the "horse that student affairs personnel rode into small colleges" (Remley, 1986). It is the prevailing factor in the small college, a place with no more people than can know each other well (Redfield, 1965). Remley (1986) believes that personalism dictates, to a certain extent, the type of person who would enjoy working in student affairs in a small college. Although administrators in both large and small institutions care about students, student-staff relationships seem more essential to the identity of student affairs staff in small colleges than in larger universities, and they remain the primary motivator and goal of the staff.

Personalism means intense involvements with faculty and staff colleagues as well. Komives (1986) and Hawley and Kuh (Chapter 2) believe that it is almost impossible not to be involved with administrators and faculty in a small college. Administrators and faculty are as visible to each other as students are to them. It is not unusual for the small college CSAO to take coffee with or attend church services with the football coach, a mathematician, the registrar, a psychology instructor, or the placement director.

Such familiarity can pose problems for some staff members. Just as students cannot hide in the back row of classes, student affairs staff cannot be shielded from criticism or approbation by a cloak of anonymity. Everyone knows the stars and the slackers—the exciting teachers, the deadwood faculty, the disinterested residence director, the great counselor or the ineffective administrator (Komives, 1986). As Goffigon, Lacey, Wright, and Kuh suggest (Chapter 7), past transgressions or indiscretions can haunt small college administrators for many years.

Effective student affairs staff members use personal knowledge of the strengths and limitations of students, faculty and colleagues when making suggestions and assigning tasks. But intense, personal relationships can also be frustrating. Informal networks both foster and frustrate change. Change may be facilitated if friends are willing to work together toward common interests. But problems may be encountered if friends are asked to support changes to which they are not committed.

Characteristics of Successful Student Affairs Staff: Multiple Roles within Multiple Service Areas

In a study of cabinet-level small college administrators, Astin and Scherrei (1980) found that CSAOs valued initiative, creativity, professional competence, effectiveness in dealing with students, interpersonal skills, and cooperation with staff members. The latter three attributes are particularly important in institutions characterized by synergy and personalism.

Interpersonal skills are the most important requirement for entry level employment in student affairs in colleges of all sizes (Ostroth, 1981). Even at the midmanagement level, communication skills are more important for employment than expertise in a particular service area (Roberts & Keys, 1983). In most institutions, however, competence increases in importance as the individual moves to higher levels of supervisory responsibility (Roberts & Keys, 1983). This might differ, perhaps, in small colleges, if individuals become supervisors of multiple functional areas. Experience within a similar institution might be as important for employment as experience within a particular functional area. At the vice-presidential level, familiarity with the type of institution is the most frequent requirement for employment, followed by interpersonal skills (Rickard, 1983).

Many small college administrators are responsible for different service areas, and most are required to serve different roles for students within any service area. This is less likely in a university where specialization includes role functions as well as functional areas. For example, a student affairs staff member in a large university might be the Assistant Director of Placement for the College of Business within an Office of Career Counseling and Placement. In the small college, that person might be the placement director and career counselor as well as an instructor in Business.

Those who work in small colleges should expect to assume three roles in addition to general administrative duties: counselor, to address personal adjustment concerns; instructor, to teach such self-help skills as study habits and stress management; and consultant, to analyze student needs and to articulate student development throughout the campus (Komives, 1984).

Counseling

Personalism is the value which integrates the different duties of the small college administrator. Personalism increases the importance of well-developed interpersonal communication skills for successful employment. Small college student affairs staff must have the capacity to establish helping relationships with students; this is far more important than clinical therapy skills which are better suited for a university counseling center role.

Small college counseling is usually more familial than formal. It has evolved from the traditional mentoring relationship between faculty and students in communities of scholars. Today, values-based, informal, counseling-oriented relationships are more prominent in small colleges than larger ones (Morrill, 1981).

In a 1983 survey of NASPA members in New England (Young, 1984), student affairs administrators affirmed that general counseling ability is more important in small colleges than technical expertise in any particular administrative area. Perhaps those administrators recognized that counseling enables administrative staff to identify appropriate services for students while it increases student involvement in the identification of their service needs. Counseling contacts encourage the integration of students with the social system of the institution, a variable positively related to retention, and retention might be the most important concern of most student affairs administrators today.

Instruction

The small college is predominantly a teaching collective (Young, 1986), and student affairs staff share teaching responsibilities. Their teaching efforts can be direct or indirect, from specific instructional assignments to teaching-related contacts outside the classroom. Morrill (1981) believes that the latter kinds of educational contacts are essential to the fulfillment of the teaching mission of a college.

The prominence of instruction (and, thus, faculty) in the small college (Walker, 1980) makes classroom teaching politically beneficial for student affairs administrators. Limited numbers of faculty make teaching opportunities more available. Many hold joint appointments in an instructional division of the college. They teach, advise, and perform other duties typically reserved for faculty in large institutions (Floyd, 1986). This can facilitate positive relations with faculty, and it should stimulate mutual staff development programs—since some faculty also have administrative responsibilities within student affairs but no formal understanding of the practices and values of the field.

Instruction beyond the classroom is also important to the small college ideology. For example, Rhatigan (1978) argued that discipline should be more than a legal process in higher education; it should be instruction in values. But in many institutions, the educative function of discipline is often underemphasized (Pavela, 1984). Small college administrators can relate discipline cases to the instructional mission of the college. This would be difficult to do in large, public institutions.

Extracurricular "instruction" earns dividends for administrators who do not teach in classrooms. Functions such as discipline might not be regarded as alien or subordinate to the instructional mission of the college. If student affairs staff can relate their activities to the instructional mission, it might boost the status and effectiveness of student affairs within the small college.

Consultation

Through consultation, the concerns and expertise of the division of student affairs can be mobilized and put into action in the institution.

In the NASPA New England survey (Young, 1984), small college practitioners reported better articulation of their concerns than administrators at larger institutions. An important target group for consultation is the faculty because the teaching mission places them, not administrators, at the center of college operations (Walker, 1980).

Astin and Scherrei (1980) reported that CSAOs are involved with faculty more than other cabinet level administrators in small colleges. They value the opinions of faculty and they have frequent transactions with them. As in any institution, faculty occasionally create consternation on the part of administrators, and are the third greatest source of frustration for student affairs vice-presidents, following administrative problems and personnel problems (Astin & Scherrei, 1980).

Current demographic conditions have made small college faculty more sensitive about the interests and concerns typically addressed by student affairs staff (Komives, 1986). Faculty recognize the importance of the freshman experience, advising, and the targeting of retention efforts. Komives advises student affairs staff to take advantage of faculty interest in these issues. They should offer retention information to faculty, orientation programs for new faculty, specialized faculty advising workshops, and pilot projects for faculty colleagues interested in innovation.

A student affairs staff member must become familiar with the characteristics of the institution and relate student affairs functions to the instructional mission of the college. Blending the disparate roles of the administrator through a transcendent purpose of student development can be politically beneficial and synergetic. Assisting with the instructional mission of the college and consulting with faculty can make the connection between student affairs and instruction obvious to all members of the campus community.

Professional Development in the Small College

Midlevel and chief student affairs administrators are interested in professional development activities which focus on their multiple role responsibilities in small colleges, job support, articulation, and financial concerns (Byrne & Rooney, 1983). Staff retreats, teamwork, and meetings are important means for fulfilling these interests (Byrne & Rooney, 1983). However, due to resource constraints, relatively few formal staff development programs are available in small colleges; therefore, informal staff development is most common (Bolles & Venter, 1979).

Graduate coursework focused on the small college is also in short supply. Seventy percent of all CSAOs who belong to NAS-

PA are employed in small colleges, but all the doctoral programs for student affairs administrators are in multiversities, the smallest of which enrolls 17,000 students (Sandeen, 1982). These institutions offer few courses that address the ideology, history, and administration of smaller colleges and universities. Increased course offerings are necessary, because familiarity with small colleges is important for advancement to a CSAO position in those institutions (Rickard, 1983).

Bossert (1983) summarized the literature on career mobility in student affairs and recommended several activities for staff enrichment and advancement, including job rotation, lateral assignments, and job sharing. He stated that the ideal work environment provides opportunities for the development of a variety of skills, identification with the whole job and not just a part of it, demonstration of the impact of the work on the lives of others, and formal and informal communication with parents, alumni, students, and faculty (Bossert, 1983). All of those elements are attainable in small college student affairs work, which mitigates some of the concerns about professional development within them.

Conclusion

Large institutions have contributed many innovations to higher education and student affairs; small colleges also have made significant contributions to the diverse system of American higher education and the quality of life. Traditionally, the small college has provided an option for student affairs administrators who want to experiment with diverse roles in different functional areas, and who are uncomfortable with the bureaucratization, specialization, and size of the multiversity. Small college student affairs staff can be innovative in ways not always possible in large university bureaucracies. They can reemphasize the centrality of student development to student affairs and they can expand its implementation through blending responsibilities for student life administration, counseling, instruction, consultation.

In the small college setting, relationships with students, faculty and other staff members are ubiquitous, and faculty relationships are especially important. Student-staff relationships demand involvement from all student affairs staff members, including the CSAO. Student affairs staff expect to become directly involved with students, to defend their services on the basis of student development, and to collaborate with faculty. To be successful, small college student affairs staff members must nurture relationships with colleagues, never forgetting that their own actions will be visible to all, and encourage students' growth and development consistent with a shared vision of the educated person.

References

Academic American Encyclopedia. (1980). Princeton: Arete Publishing Company.

Astin, A. W. (1984) Student involvement: A developmental theory for higher education. *Journal of College Student Personnel, 25,* 297-308.

Astin, A. W., & Scherrei, R. (1980). *Maximizing leadership effectiveness.* San Francisco: Jossey-Bass.

Bolles, L., & Venter, D. (1979). Student personnel and the small residential college. *Journal of College Student Personnel, 19,* 272.

Bossert, R. (1983, March). Career mobility in student affairs. In Evans, N. and Bossert, R. *The status of preparation, employment opportunities and advancement in the field of student affairs* (pp. IV 1-36). Preliminary report for the ACPA Commission XII Research Committee.

Brown, R. D. (1972). *Student development in tomorrow's higher education—A return to the academy.* Washington: American College Personnel Association.

Byrne, R. (1984). Small college task force progress report. *NASPA Forum, 4(7),* 8-9.

Byrne, R., & Rooney, P. (1983). *Small college survey of chief student affairs officers and mid-level management professionals.* Mimeographed report for NASPA Small College Task Force, Mount Holyoke College.

Floyd, D. (1980). Chief student affairs administrators in public, small and rural community colleges: A profile. *The Southern College Personnel Association Journal, 3(1),* 25-34.

Floyd, D. (1986). A community college reaction. *Journal of College Student Personnel, 27,* 10-12.

Komives, S. (1986). Each small college has a story to tell. *Journal of College Student Personnel, 27,* 13-15.

Komives, S. (1984, June 29). *The cult of the true believers.* Paper presented at the NASPA Symposium on Student Development, Brunswick, ME.

Morrill, R. (1981). *Teaching values in college.* San Francisco: Jossey-Bass.

Ostroth, D. (1981). Competencies for entry-level professionals: What do employers look for when hiring new staff? *Journal of College Student Personnel. 22,* 5-11.

Pavela, G. (1984, June). Editor's column. *ACPA Commission XV News*, 1-4.

Redfield, R. (1965). The folk society. In T. Lasswell (Ed.), *Life in society* (pp. 320-328). Chicago: Scott, Foresman.

Remley, A. (1986). Real vs. ideal — A response. *Journal of College Student Personnel, 27*, 16-17.

Rhatigan, J. (1978). A corrective look back. In Appleton, J., Briggs, C. and Rhatigan, J., (Eds.), *Pieces of eight* (pp. 9-41). Portland: NIRAD.

Rickard, S. (1983). Institutional requirements for chief student affairs officers. *NASPA Forum, 4*(2), 6-7.

Riesman, D. (1981). *On higher education.* San Francisco: Jossey-Bass.

Roberts, D., & Keys, A. (1983, March). *Student personnel hiring practices.* Paper presented at the meeting of the American College Personnel Association, Houston, TX.

Sandeen, A. (1982). Professional preparation programs in student personnel services in higher education: A national assessment by chief student affairs officers. *NASPA Journal, 20*(2), 51-58.

Walker, D. (1981). The president as ethical leader of the campus. In Baca, M. and Stein, R. (Eds.). *Professional ethics in university administration* (pp. 14-28). San Francisco: Jossey-Bass, New Directions for Higher Education.

Wrenn, C. G.(1967). The development of student personnel work in the United States and some guidelines for the future. In J. Minter (Ed.), *The individual and the system* (pp. 101-121). Boulder: W.I.C.H.E.

Young, R. (1984). *Survey of characteristics of NASPA members in New England.* Burlington, VT: University of Vermont.

Young, R. (1986). The small college point of view: An ideology of student affairs. *Journal of College Student Personnel, 27*, 4-9.

Chapter 6

The View from the Top: The Small College Chief Student Affairs Officer's Experience

David P. Dodson, Patricia M. Volp, and Andrea C. McAleenan

The purpose of this chapter is to describe, from a personal point of view, the chief student affairs officer's (CSAO) role in a small college setting. This profile of the CSAO role is a composite of the experiences of three people who have been Deans of Students at small colleges in the Northeast, the Midwest, and the Northwest. Each contributor has between ten and twenty years of professional experience to draw upon in their reflections. The journey to the deanship, the daily challenges, and the unique opportunities for college wide impact are discussed. Common threads emerge from the experiences of the three contributors which lends credence to the notion that small college deans share a similar set of challenges and opportunities.

Three Paths to the Small College CSAO Position

Between the completion of my course work and defending my Ph.D. dissertation in Philosophy, I considered several career options, in large part because of my anxiety about the prospect of ever finding a permanent teaching post. After talking with people in the field and thinking about the incredible burdens assigned to student affairs personnel, I concluded that student "deaning" was too often a thankless job. Thus, I chose to be a professor of philosophy in a small liberal arts college.

However, soon after the arrival of a new president of the college, I was faced with one of those life-changing, momentous decisions. The president asked if I would consider applying for the position of dean. "Oh, no," I replied, "I enjoy teaching too much to consider such a move. Besides, I really don't feel I have the background or the inclination to take on the enormous chores of operating a student affairs division." The president was undaunted. He indicated that he sought a close connection between the academic concerns of the institution and campus life. I was intrigued by the challenge, and after a few days' reflection I decided to submit my name in application.

I accepted the offer on a one-year trial basis. Ten years later, I am happy to report that I have found my concerns about in-depth student contact totally allayed. I have discovered that, as the CSAO, I meet students from all disciplines at important, life-changing moments in their college careers. Many times these encounters take place in the midst of a crisis or during a personal triumph. I find the opportunity to serve as a support and guide to students who have great potential but are suffering momentary reversals, to be thoroughly satisfying.

After experience in a wide variety of fields: public relations, student activities, career counseling, admissions work in a Catholic girls high school, and some college-level teaching, I decided to complete my doctoral studies in higher education. My formal education was in journalism, organizational behavior, and student personnel administration. I decided the broad field of higher education would be perfect for blending my academic background and interests. I answered the advertisement for the chief student affairs administrator since it fit in with my educational philosophy, the college was in my home state, and the setting complemented my Catholic educational background and experience.

Despite a long standing commitment to the performing arts, I was drawn to the profession of student affairs by my work as a resident assistant and the advice of my mentor in student affairs. He challenged me to explore the potential of the contribution I could make by focusing my energies on the holistic development of students; I found myself entering a student personnel administration masters program, a far cry from the undergraduate major I had pursued. From the beginning of my experience, the generalist roots that I now profess are basic characteristics of successful staff at small colleges began to take hold. I tried to learn everything I could about all phases of student affairs work and throughout the first ten years of my career I worked in almost every area of student affairs. Although I worked primarily on large campuses in three different states in the early years of my career, the broad exposure to institution-wide concerns enabled me to develop my philosophy about the potential of holistic student affairs work on a small college campus. I decided a small college was an ideal environment to implement a holistic student development philosophy and programming. I tested that theory in the role of professor, director of a graduate student affairs preparation program, and dean of instruction on a small college campus prior to becoming dean of students on another campus across the country.

Through these cameos a common theme emerges. Each of us was attracted by the opportunity to bring a holistic perspective into our life work. We came to see that it is possible to inspire students to embark on journeys that they never dreamed would be theirs. Initially we were thrilled by the train of students who passed through our lives evidencing some form of personal growth. But then we began to realize the challenge for remolding an institution so that its potential for influencing students' lives could be even greater. By reflecting and strategizing about institutional steps which could be taken to make the college more congruent with its professed aims of producing teaching and learning of the highest order, a new intellectual challenge was undertaken.

The Scope of the Job

A typical day in the life of a dean on a small college campus is hectic, and includes meetings with a variety of individuals and groups, preparation for upcoming meetings and presentations, phone contact with students, parents, administration, and faculty, and attendance at various student activities and athletic events. The eternal frustration is the stack of uncompleted work and correspondence that must often go unattended because of the intense demands for "people time."

The following list is illustrative of the range of issues with which deans at small colleges must cope on a daily basis: meeting with the director of residence life and the vice president for finance to discuss housing arrangements; an appointment with the director of counseling to design group sessions for the semester (eating disorders, homesickness, depression, substance abuse); meeting with a student planning to withdraw from the college to determine reasons for leaving that will be included in the information base for the new retention program; meeting with the registrar and academic dean to design next year's calendar; meeting with the publications staff and director of orientation to discuss publications for next year; and, finally, dinner with student government officers to establish goals for the year and to help formulate a plan for revision of their constitution. Each requires the ability to shift gears rapidly and think holistically.

Direct student contact is a high priority, particularly with the leadership of student groups. This enables the dean to gain a clearer understanding of student perceptions and problems in order to anticipate and respond to situations prior to a crisis emerging. Direct student contact is the very best way to communicate a philosophy of student development to the entire campus.

One of the most important aspects in the life of a dean is the selection, training, and supervision of staff. Student affairs staff are the "on-line people" who actually give the philosophy and vision of the dean and the division its life and breath. To respond to this challenge, the dean must be able to create a close knit team where communication, openness, and vulnerability are modeled and affirmed. A staff committed to the mission of the college and the student affairs division can be a dynamic, energetic force for creating the most positive learning environment possible for students. If the Dean of Students is able to inspire and affirm his or her staff, the staff—in turn—will do the same for the students with whom they work. It is a matter of putting beliefs and theory into practice.

One of the advantages of being a dean at a small college is that it is possible to design programs and events that involve virtually all students. Whether it be all-campus variety shows, freshman assessment surveys, or student development portfolios, the personalism and holistic nature of small colleges is evident. At a small college a dean actually has the opportunity to work one-on-one with students to influence growth. Although a similar opportunity is available at larger universities, the difference may be most significantly noted in the amount and type of direct student contact. At large universities, the dean may come into contact with a small proportion of the student body, usually only the most motivated students or the ones in severe difficulty. At small colleges the dean interacts with a cross section of students on an ongoing basis.

The job is overwhelming on occasion, always unpredictable, but profoundly challenging and deeply satisfying. The CSAO's position is never boring and provides wonderfully quick turnaround time from planning to action. The challenge is to be ready at the right place at the right time with the right plan.

The diversity of staff and program responsibilities is frequently the most challenging aspect of a dean's work. (Maybe it is a job for people who become bored easily.) In addition to the mainstays of student affairs (e.g., residence life, admissions, financial aids, career centers, student activities, orientation, athletics, and student government), student affairs work on small college campuses is always carving new directions in response to student interests and needs. Wellness programs, freshman convocations, ongoing orientation programs, athletic and activity clubs, off campus service projects, and student leadership classes are but a few of the opportunities available to encourage students' growth. These programs have various degrees of turnaround time from planning to implementation. The magic is that the initiative from students, either in terms of ideas expressed or needs assessed, prompts the action.

Staff development can be both a joy and a frustration. Limited funds require creative programming designed to take advantage of on-campus talent or professional colleagues from nearby campuses in the role of consultant or mentor. The dean has the responsibility to create the tone and priority for a personal and professional development program on campus through role modeling a commitment to growth in his or her own life. Through conversation and observation, staff members begin to see the importance of keeping alive and up-to-date professionally and for establishing goals and plans for the year.

Another challenge in this position is that most student affairs staff at small colleges are not employed during the summer. Consequently, although summers are an ideal time for planning and decision-making, the process is difficult without the ability to consult and involve staff. The need to have staff as a central part of new programs and policies can be short-circuited without factoring in this scheduling dimension.

One effective strategy may be to set aside time prior to the opening of school in the fall for a full staff retreat off campus. During this time, each staff member prepares a ten-minute presentation covering personal and professional goals for the coming year. Other staff members have the opportunity to respond to the person and encourage those efforts by offering feedback and support. At the same time, the dean can provide personal affirmation to each person on staff by responding directly to the plans after each presentation. The dean can also make a presentation on the state of student development which may serve as a springboard for discussion on the center's directions and plans for the year. This format can help to create a spirit of unity for the entire year.

Through sharing and discussing information institution-wide, a student affairs staff can gain consensus on ways that student affairs programs and services can enhance the entire campus. This process becomes foundational for prioritizing specific student development programs and strategies. When a staff feels they are a central part of the establishment of goals, they are more likely to make a personal commitment to reaching them. This process can be followed by regular staff meetings devoted to monitoring and evaluating progress toward the agreed upon goals for the year.

One additional variable with which many small college CSAOs must deal is the incredibly slight margin of error. In a small college driven by tuition revenue, attrition can be a major pressure, and a small number of students withdrawing can have drastic effects on the institution's budget. Presidents often expect student affairs staff to take responsibility for retention. This type of institution-wide concern demands everyone's involvement and is one of the most significant ways for student affairs to demonstrate campus-wide leadership.

Hazards for Small-College Deans

There are moments, of course, when every dean may have second thoughts and wonder, "What if I would have chosen a different career?" Such moments almost always occur when some unexpected reversal has prevented the institution or a particular idea from becoming what it might become. For example, many of us have experienced the trauma of not having an entering freshman class as large as expected. Consequently, the projected budgets required considerable paring which usually proves to be a grueling experience for everyone involved.

When an institution suffers reversal, the pressures placed upon people in its human service delivery system are enormous. A great toll is taken in human energy and considerable harm often occurs to individuals at such times. At those times, a superhuman amount of energy is required to keep the staff and students motivated and positively looking forward. The dean cannot afford to suffer any delusions about the amount of power. The dean can assist in the forward movement of the institution, but is successful only to the extent that the organization itself is sound and vigorous.

Although small colleges have the reputation for being creative laboratories, capable of testing student development theories, sometimes there is a definite conflict between crisis management and proactive programming. The student affairs staff is often so overloaded with committee assignments and paperwork, that they have little time for inspirational moments to spark the implementation of new ideas. Instead, they become maintenance oriented—responding only to crises at hand.

Another challenge is that the majority of paperwork—reports and correspondence—goes home with deans. Days are generally booked solid between committee and council meetings, interaction with staff members, and appointments with students. Drop-ins consume the few idle moments available. Those times can be extremely effective in terms of keeping an open door to staff members who need to consult on matters in between official appointments or regular staff meetings. The position seems to have an uncanny characteristic of acquiring more and more work until there are no daylight hours to complete it. Advocates of time management theory would insist on scheduling work time with no meetings or interruptions; however, efforts in this regard always go down the drain when a student shows up with a crisis or a staff member absolutely must check something prior to making a decision. The small college atmosphere often sets a dean up for guilt by nonassociation. All of the above could be easier to handle if student affairs staff as a whole weren't so overloaded. Usually another time management strategy, "delegation," is simply not feasible.

Other parts of the not-so-rosy side of the CSAO role are exemplified by the goldfish-bowl syndrome. It is not unusual for *any* member of this "friendly, close community" to regularly offer suggestions about how the student affairs area can function better. A small college dean receives an inordinate am-mount of feedback regularly. The position also puts one into a very narrow social sphere. Everyone knows everything about the dean's so-called "private" life. Besides working crazy hours and attending unending rounds of campus activities—to show support for the *students,* the dean is also expected to keep up on the literature and contribute professionally.

There seems to be a universally held belief on small college campuses that you have to put in twice as much effort as you are paid for. This endless round of activities can spill into the family also. While a small college environment can be an ideal climate in which to raise children due to opportunities for extensive informal interactions and stimulating cultural, spiritual, athletic, and social activities, the expectations for the whole family to be involved can be an additional pressure requiring close communication and agreement with one's spouse. If a mutually acceptable plan is not agreed upon, this pressure point can produce ongoing friction.

Some feel that the CSAO in a small college setting is expected to be a woman or man for all seasons. The pressures are intense if you buy into this requirement. Careful reflection and clear action based on personal and family priorities are important ground rules to establish. Surrounding oneself with some key support people is another basic survival necessity that cannot be overlooked.

Advice from Small College CSAOs

It is important to give one's best intellectual and personal energies to strengthen and encourage the development of students' integrity and vision, and in so doing promote excellence throughout the college. The CSAO has the opportunity to serve as the institution's conscience or, at least, as its ombudsman. The dean, in effect, operates at the heart and soul level of the institution. Through a distinctive style of administration—the decisions made or words of support or chastisement—the CSAO has an opportunity to express in vivid life-changing ways the human side of an institution. Thus, although the dean's influence may be difficult to discern on first glance, over the course of time, the CSAO is one of the most important, influential persons in the college.

A critical question is whether one can be authentic in a particular environment. Does the institution free you to use your strengths and gifts? You need to be sure what the college actually wants done. Do the actual day-to-day operations match the catalogue rhetoric? Is there a climate of readiness and openness to change? Can one actually implement a student development philosophy? What external pressures can be expected from the board of trustees, parents, and the community both on and off campus? Is there a five-year plan that the dean is expected to implement or can you blaze your own trail?

All of these issues are important since each individual needs to have a sense of purpose for investing in this arena where intrinsic rewards are more attainable than extrinsic rewards in most cases. Even then, only occasionally does one get from another some sense that he or she is doing a first rate job. But once in awhile deans receive some feedback on a situation that keeps them going. For example, in one case a dean received a letter from a student who had received disciplinary sanctions for a violation of regulations. The student stated that while he was not pleased with the decision, he respected it and, furthermore, he was grateful that he had received a thorough explanation of why the sanction was necessary. He said, "I think you have been firm but fair." This response reveals that he had experienced a larger sense of the need for more responsible concern for the welfare of others. On other occasions deans of students receive, especially from parents, expressions of appreciation for the role they have played in providing support and continuing direction for their children. Without these moments the CSAO role would be sterile.

The CSAO and staff can model the virtues of liberal education by exhibiting maturity, adaptability, allocentrism, and love of life, the peculiar qualities of a "high impact" college. By embracing individual and social diversity, the dean can seek ways to challenge stereotypic thinking and to reduce the ethnic, political, cultural, and social barriers within the college or university that make some students wary about learning from people whom they regard as different in important respects. Effective CSAOs are collaborators, referral agents and above all, team-players who attempt to establish and maintain networks of faculty, administrators, and students. Such networks are shaped by a common commitment to an integrative educational experience. We can also be catalysts for institutional innovation and experimentation; by personal example we must model effective leadership. We should be secure enough to permit students to take appropriate responsibility and, when merited, receive all the credit for it.

Conclusion

The CSAO position takes its toll on physical and personal energies, but at the same time it can be regenerative and challenging. As we have observed and experienced the challenges of the position and the problems which confront small colleges, we know that physical energy, emotional sensitivity and stability, intellectual capacity, and perseverance are qualities that we all strive for and yet fall short of so frequently.

An effective CSAO does not depend primarily upon financial resources, or large numbers of staff, or well-publicized programs, although all of these may be important secondary factors. We believe an effective CSAO provides direction to a team of people who share a common mission. When a student development staff exhibits the characteristics mentioned above, an institution can be profoundly affected.

Chapter 7

The Small College Experience: The Generalist's Perspective

Rob Goffigon, Debra Lacey, Janet R. Wright, and George D. Kuh

This chapter describes the ethos of student affairs work in a small college from the generalist's point of view. The presentation reflects the striking similarities in the personal experiences of three student affairs workers. Their contributions were edited to create a composite portrait of the life of the small college student affairs worker. They range in age from mid-20s to early 30s, and have from three to six years of experience in student affairs work. Two of the three individuals have baccalaureate degrees from small colleges. All earned masters degrees with an emphasis in student development.

What Is Attractive About Student Affairs Work in a Small College Setting

As an undergraduate at a small college, college administration was not a serious career option. But during those years significant personal growth occurred and a new awareness of potential emerged. During graduate school, the commitment to small college student affairs work was crystallized; working in this type of institution provides an opportunity to complete the generative loop, to contribute to and maintain a community of faith and learning that nurtures personal and spiritual growth.

It is common, especially on primarily residential campuses, to hear faculty, student affairs staff, and students describe themselves in terms of family or "community." Community is fostered when students know classmates, are acquainted with people in other classes, are free to say "hi" to anyone on the campus simply because they are on the campus and, therefore, part of their world. Some people might view the smiles, the "hellos," the nods of recognition, or the brief chats on the sidewalk as tedious or superficial. But this openness and recognition of others breathes life into the community. Community also means coming to know professors as persons, perhaps even on a first name basis, through the central purpose of the institution—teaching. Another advantage is the close working relationship between faculty and staff that tends to characterize small colleges. Student affairs staff are usually invited to attend faculty meetings and annual faculty retreats. Because faculty at small colleges tend to take a personal interest in students, they also seem to be more willing to work with the student affairs staff in responding to students' needs and concerns. It sometimes takes time to educate the faculty about student affairs philosophy and purposes. The response may be slow, but it is usually positive. Taking a personal interest in faculty also underscores the commonalities between the goals of the faculty and the student affairs mission. These are advantages to students and to student affairs staff.

The small college gives student affairs staff numerous opportunities to participate in students' growth, and sometimes for staff to share their development with students. Many students at small colleges expect a more personalized experience and to communicate more frequently and more openly with faculty and staff. The extent to which openness and personal contact encourage development is not always clear, but these conditions certainly *seem* compatible with human development goals.

The ethos of the small college values people as individuals.

Not only students but faculty and staff seem appreciated more for their unique talents and skills. The self-selection process that draws faculty, staff, and students to small colleges says something about their values and priorities (e.g., people are more important than the reputation of the institution, high salaries, or status).

The Upside and Downside of Multiple Roles

Entry level position descriptions at small colleges suggest that student affairs staff should not expect to sleep very much. Jobs are often designed as a combination of two or more halftime positions, such as housing director and career counselor. The former might include room assignments, student conduct, training and supervision of residence life staff, dorm councils, student judicial boards, and the usual assortment of activities which comfortably fall under the heading of "crisis management;" the latter role may include implementing the college's career development program, often without any budget to speak of. Over the course of the academic year, additional assignments might be added (e.g., study skills class, counseling for students admitted on academic probation), and it is not unusual to become involved in student organizations and clubs as well.

A "generalist" must wear many "hats;" the hats often must be changed about every hour which leads to some frustrations and more than a little pressure. Quick adjustments and unexpected transitions are common; no two days are exactly alike. This is probably true at large institutions as well, but there is so much less specialization in a small college setting that this issue is built into the numerous roles that are required of staff. But playing multiple roles has advantages because they: (1) provide a good sense of the broader student development mission; (2) permit staff to interact with different types of students and staff; and (3) encourage autonomy which permits staff to select interesting things to do.

Exhaustion often accompanies multiple roles and responsibilities. One must guard against developing the grand delusion of being a superstar or a "hero." Those who begin to believe it, usually fall victim to feelings of burnout, disillusionment, and guilt in trying to play the role. Recognizing and learning how to work within limitations can ameliorate the "burnout" tendency, a continual concern among small college student affairs staff.

The lack of time to adequately prepare for every meeting or situation can occasionally lead to guilt, or at least feeling less capable and confident than is desirable. Sometimes effectiveness and quality must be sacrificed for coverage. The best strategy is to develop organizational skills in the areas of scheduling, record keeping, and information management. It is a mistake to think that since student affairs is a "person-oriented" profession, filing, record keeping, or cataloging systems are not important. It doesn't take long to learn that forms, reports, records, correspondence, and resource materials are peculiar to each area of responsibility. A few extra evening hours spent designing a system for processing and maintaining that information is time well invested.

Scheduling can be a real nemesis. In the first few months on the job, it may seem that every available time slot on the calendar should be filled with *something*. It takes awhile to realize the importance of reserving time for planning, reflection, and refining new ideas. When it becomes clear that "just one more commitment" might seriously jeopardize the effectiveness of another program, saying "no" without guilt becomes easier to do. Therefore, time management also is important; but time management is based in part on the autonomy to establish priorities, which in student affairs work is at times beyond one's control. Priorities are often set by others at higher levels of responsibility in the college, and not always in one's order of preference.

Personal and Professional Tradeoffs

There is a lot of room for initiative and creativity in the small college setting, and one can usually expect support for good ideas, once the ideas have been discussed. An individual staff member can make a real difference in a relatively short period of time. With the support of the dean and the student affairs committee, and with input from a number of students, residence life staff members, and faculty, a first year staff member can implement a redesigned student-based judicial board within a year's time. Such overhauls are not without problems and criticisms, of course, but major procedural transformations can be initiated by a first year staff member. Whether a first year staff member could have that degree of influence in a larger institution is doubtful. What makes such a change possible is the opportunity for developing close personal working relationships with faculty, students, staff, and administrators. Sometimes the close physical proximity of offices can provide opportunities for frequent, casual contact. People can become personally acquainted with staff and also become sensitive to the context in which a program is being developed.

Faculty and students come to know student affairs staff as persons, and they come to value one's skills and abilities. With a reasonable amount of knowledge and expertise, a student affairs staff member can feel very important on a small campus; and feeling important and appreciated is a wonderful feeling, both personally and professionally. It is not unusual for faculty to pass along compliments to staff based on the positive things they have heard from students they have in class.

Another advantage of student affairs work in the small college setting is the potential for a close, tightknit working relationship among the staff. At many small colleges, it is relatively easy for all the student development staff to meet periodically as a group which encourages collaboration and mutual support. As a result, the working environment encourages staff unity, provided personality conflicts and communication problems can be handled effectively.

Working in the "Fishbowl"

A large institution offers considerable anonymity; on a small college campus, flaws are magnified. Accordingly, there are sometimes unpleasant consequences to being well known in a setting where mistakes are just as visible as successes. Gossip and rumor mills are by no means unique to the small institution, yet when coupled with the "fishbowl" qualities of this environment, these effects seem all the more devastating. There is literally no refuge from the curiosity, insinuations, and speculations generated by information transmitted through broken confidences and muted asides.

In an "upclose and personal climate," staff are well known, and the reputation of an ineffective staff member can haunt the entire student development division. Every staff member experiences some of the consequences of students' dislike or disrespect for one of the staff. And even after the staff person is gone, skepticism may linger. There are no winners in this situation; everybody suffers including the persons spreading rumors and the individuals who are the target of the rumors. In fact, one of the great challenges of working in a small college is to maintain personal credibility and integrity when exchanging information about colleagues and students.

Because of the informal, flexible atmosphere in many small colleges, pressure may be intense for upper level administrators to be effective leaders. When leadership fails and communication breaks down, staff can become very resentful and critical. In fact, there may be more pressure in the small college environment to be competent both personally and professionally since both the personal and professional aspects of performance are visible to many members of the community.

Small colleges have a way of maintaining tradition; sometimes the "institutional saga" impedes change. Some faculty and administrators just recently have come to the realization that many nontraditional students are beginning to come to college. Consequently, student affairs staff must work very hard to remain current with information about the needs of today's and tomorrow's college student, and to communicate this information to faculty colleagues.

Another problem is the lack of resources to support professional development; there seems to be little time and money allocated for these activities. In fact, the budget line item often first to be reduced is "professional development," whether off-campus opportunities, like conventions and workshops, or on-campus meetings and retreats. Professional development is expected to come out of personal time and finances. Nonetheless, professional development opportunities are very important for motivation and effectiveness. Thus, one has to capitalize on regional conferences and look to colleagues for stimulation. But at many conferences it appears that program topics are biased toward the larger institution, and understandably so. Hopefully, that will change as more small college staff members become involved in the professional associations.

Having a satisfactory personal life in a small town can be a particularly challenging and difficult aspect of the job. In most small towns there are very few people around in their early 30s to seek out for friendship and recreation. Some staff look forward to leaving the campus for a weekend (much like students!) to be with friends for stimulation and intellectual challenge. This can be a difficult adjustment if one is without personal support sources, professional stimulation, and staff members from whom one can learn and respect. It also is difficult to tolerate the sexism and racism that is common to some small, rural towns.

Personal and Professional Growth

Many student affairs staff enter graduate programs in student development right after graduating from college. As a result, they tend to be relatively young and insecure about their skills and abilities when they assume their first position. Many are reserved and may be reluctant to share their thinking with colleagues due to feelings of intimidation. Some believe they lack the experience to make a significant contribution to the welfare of students and the life of the college. But after a few years in the field considerable growth typically takes place in self-confidence. One's inner core of values, that lends direction to behavior, becomes better clarified. Most staff are better skilled and more comfortable speaking in front of groups and sharing information with faculty and students' parents.

While knowledge and training are important, most staff do not always use their skills and knowledge to full advantage. Over time, expectations of co-workers tend to increase and staff also become less tolerant of incompetence displayed by those with whom one works, especially colleagues within the student development program.

In spite of high expectations for personal and colleague performance, one may become less of a perfectionist about many things. Showing humanness when appropriate is critical. It is amazing how significant it is for students to hear a staff member say, "I am sorry," and to ask them for forgiveness. Students need to see an administrator's humanness and frailties. They need to have a glimpse of the professional's own account of personal growth.

Many students at small colleges are eager to learn more about themselves, and gravitate toward people and programs that foster self-discovery. Therefore, it is not unusual for personal development groups to be in demand, particularly if group activities are specifically suited to the needs of students. Some group work training is available in graduate school, but typically more emphasis is placed on task-oriented groups as opposed to growth groups; certainly this is true in administration as compared with counseling oriented preparation programs.

Student affairs staff enjoy a considerable degree of autonomy, and one must learn how to handle autonomy without abusing the confidence of colleagues. A basic understanding of student development theory and how to translate theory is invaluable. From this knowledge comes a sense of things that need to be done, improved upon, or implemented in order to increase one's effectiveness. Through experience one also learns not to overevaluate programs. Especially with orientation programs, there comes a time to weigh the criticisms and to recognize that there may not be a way to ameliorate some of the problems without jeopardizing the integrity and value of other aspects of the program.

After a few years, volunteerism decreases and the importance placed on team work, camaraderie, and the pursuit of common goals increases; the need for personal achievement seems to diminish. Learning about, and showing appreciation for, tasks performed well by other people also becomes more important. An appreciation develops for discretion and integrity in the sharing of information, for personal and professional flexibility, and for the capacity to deal with uncertainty and ambiguity. But one becomes a bit more cautious as well. In the small college "fishbowl," student affairs staff must be sensitive to words, actions, opinions, and even personal relationships. Therefore, selectivity in self-disclosure and in what one does with free time seems to increase. It is essential to have some time to regenerate personal energy stores. College age students, especially in counseling situations, can be very draining, and it is important to replenish energy after a hard week.

Persons considering a generalist position in a small college, should learn as much as possible about the people with whom and for whom they will be working, and make certain that these are folks they can enjoy, respect, and learn from. Estimate the potential for a personal life, especially if the college is in a small town. Are there any likely mentors and what are the possibilities for friends and colleagues? Are professional and personal growth encouraged and supported, and how? What is a realistic amount of time to remain in the position and what is a logical next move when it's time to leave? Finally, set some long and short range goals and keep them clearly in mind to get through the bad days.

Without question, large campuses have an energy and diversity that cannot be matched by small colleges. But it is easy to deeply appreciate and respect the unique qualities of the small college—where people think in terms of "community." A great sense of satisfaction can be derived from working with colleagues, some of whom will become close personal friends. An equally important source of satisfaction can be derived from challenging students' thinking and encouraging them to think about themselves and the world differently. The small college setting allows student affairs staff to see students in sometimes very personal ways, and to know them long enough and well enough to observe growth and change taking place. Students often reflect on the ways in which they have grown and changed, and it is personally gratifying to see a student graduate who has developed a strong sense of worth and direction from experiencing student life in college. This is what makes student affairs work rewarding, both professionally and personally, and is the legacy that one generation of students and student affairs staff passes on to the next generation.

A clear vision of one's life work demands time, patience, support, and the nourishment of others. The longer one is in this business, the clearer one's vision becomes. In the small college, student affairs staff need to lift each other up, support each other, and fight hard not to let the vision fade . . . The small college is a place for dreamers, and dreams give birth to purpose and direction.

Small colleges have a special place and purpose in higher education. And the student affairs generalist has a very special place on the small college campus.

Chapter 8

The Future of Student Affairs Work in Small Colleges

George D. Kuh and Andrea C. McAleenan

Four themes characteristic of student affairs work in small colleges reverberate throughout this monograph and are summarized in the first section of this chapter. Then, three conditions common to many small colleges that bode well for the future of student affairs work are discussed. Finally, a modest student affairs agenda is proposed that takes advantage of these conditions to further the aims of the small college.

Characteristics of Student Affairs Work in Small Colleges

Student affairs workers can expect to perform *multiple roles* as they become *involved* in virtually every facet of the small college community. Typically, student affairs staff *collaborate* with faculty and others in encouraging students' development consistent with student's hopes and dreams *and* with the institution's mission. Equally important, small college student affairs workers recognize that *meaningful, personal relationships* with students and colleagues are necessary to encourage human development in the academy.

Multiple Roles

As underscored by Goffigon, Lacey, Wright, and Kuh (Chapter 7), the nature of the small college requires staff to be multi-faceted, to perform two or more primary roles (e.g., director of residence life and career advisor), each of which in larger institutions may be the responsibility of one or more staff. As a result of performing multiple roles, the small college staff member learns more about the institutional culture, faculty, and students than a staff member in a more specialized role on a larger campus because he or she is required to deal with different kinds of problems. According to Dodson, Volp, and McAleenan (Chapter 6), the CSAO also must wear multiple hats. The CSAO sets the tone, establishes the priorities, and demonstrates a working model for the campus community. The CSAO must be a multi-talented, multi-skilled individual with the ability to see the whole institutional context and orchestrate responses to student and faculty needs within a campus-wide framework while remaining sensitive to competing pressures from other constituencies including alumni and townspeople.

Student affairs staff in smaller institutions may know people better and, therefore, develop a more comprehensive picture of the overall context of the institution than their counterparts at a larger institution. But multiple role expectations require a great tolerance for ambiguity and a high frustration threshold. Small college student affairs staff must be comfortable with the work scope of a generalist; this does not preclude specialized interests, of course, but it may often require compromising personal or professional growth agendas in order to champion the goals of the student development program within the context of the institution's mission.

Involvement

Involvement seems to be a catchword in the academy. During the past several years, the higher education literature has been replete with references to the importance of students' involvement in various facets of campus life and the relationship between involvement and satisfaction, achievement, and persistence to graduation (Astin, 1977, 1984, 1985; Kuh, 1981; Pace,

1982; Pascarella, 1980; Study Group on the Conditions of Excellence in American Higher Education, 1984). A high level of involvement also seems to be necessary for effective student affairs work in the small college setting.

The nature of the small college environment precludes student or staff anonymity, and demands that staff in particular be actively engaged in their specific assignments as well as other dimensions of campus life such as student advising and counseling, fund raising, curriculum revision, and alumni relations. Student affairs workers who wish to focus on specific concerns (e.g., therapy to ameliorate depression) of a relatively small number of students are not likely to be satisfied on a small college campus where active participation in daily routines and major campus events is expected of everyone. Equally important, involvement in various aspects of campus life mediates *collaboration* with colleagues.

Collaboration

Performing multiple roles and being integrated into the social and academic fabric of the institution is facilitated through networking and collaboration with students, student affairs colleagues, and faculty. The underpopulated small college environment demands that individuals work together to perform the variety of tasks required to maintain a productive, satisfying living-learning community.

Collaboration requires confident, mature student affairs staff secure in their primary roles and willing to expand their professional identity by performing instructional roles characteristic of faculty and learner roles characteristic of students. In fact, one of the great attractions about the small college environment is that the demand for and encouragement of collaboration provides continuing personal and professional challenges to all members of the community including student affairs staff. This is exactly the converse of a stereotypical view of the small college held by many; i.e., a static, cloistered tradition-bound academy in which clear, narrow role definitions result in repetitive, standardized, almost routine behaviors. Creative, enterprising staff can transform the small college into an opportunity-rich, environment in which students and others recognize the importance of shared visions to a liberating education and can pursue personal growth agendas.

Personalism

Perhaps the most distinctive quality of small colleges is the genuine interest that faculty and staff take in students and each other. Compared with their counterparts at larger institutions, students at liberal arts colleges perceive a "sense of community," and believe faculty take a personal interest in them, both in and out of the classroom (Carnegie Foundation for the Advancement of Teaching, 1985). According to Young (Chapter 5), "personalism means intense involvements with faculty and staff as well."

The small college campus is distinctive when it is a caring, personalized community that recognizes the needs and responsibilities of all members, sometimes in painful ways. Just as students cannot remain anonymous, neither can student affairs staff. The "fishbowl-like" sensation described by the contributors to Chapter 6 and Chapter 7 underscores the importance of role modeling to maintaining a clear, coherent sense of purpose. At its best, the small college is a supportive, nurturing environment in which participants know they are important to others and to themselves.

These characteristics are not solely a function of size; as McAleenan and Kuh suggested in Chapter 1, students' perceptions are as important as physical parameters of the campus or numbers of students. And yet, for a long time, the folklore of higher education has underscored physical and numerical indices as distinctive characteristics of quality in higher education. Anecdotal reports by student affairs staff (Chapters 5, 6 and 7) and empirical data (Carnegie Foundation for the Advancement of Teaching, 1985) suggest certain aspects of this folklore are true. Small colleges can be unique, developmentally powerful environments, not only for students but also for student affairs staff.

Positive Conditions for Student Affairs Work

Three conditions of small college environments bode well for the future of student affairs work. *First,* small colleges—like their larger counterparts—are in desperate need of leadership from within. The past two decades have been characterized by increasing external influence over IHEs. Like special interest groups that have made political consensus almost impossible to attain at the national level (Reich, 1983), external influences on IHEs (e.g., state regulatory bodies such as commissions on higher education, state legislators, federal program initiatives) often provide little assistance in solving campus problems; rather, the increasingly complex policies and procedures requested by regulatory agencies sometimes immobilize many IHEs from responding with verve and a sense of purpose to the fiscal and philosophical challenges facing contemporary higher education.

On a small campus, one person with vision, compassion, energy, and good ideas can make a difference. Of course, this person does not have to be a student affairs staff member. But other factors are at work on the small campus that make the CSAO or another student affairs staff member a likely leader. For example, considerable attention is now focused on enrollment management, not only as a marketing or new student recruitment and retention strategy (Hossler, 1984), but also as an institutional renewal program that welcomes participation by faculty, students, staff, alumni, and administrators. Enrollment management underscores the need for collaboration and involvement of peers, faculty, and others on the campus. In this sense, enrollment management is an institutional learning device whereby: (a) faculty become aware of the perceptions of their disciplines held by prospective, current, and former students; (b) administrators come to grips with the strengths and weaknesses of the college as perceived by on-campus and off-campus groups; and (c) student affairs staff receive feedback about the link between maintaining a secure, pleasant living environment and students' achievement and satisfaction. A comprehensive enrollment management strategy focuses on what must be done by faculty and student affairs staff to attract and retain highly motivated, able students.

Enrollment management is *au courant*. But the concept does illustrate the need for leadership by a small group of individuals who share a vision and a rich understanding of the institution's heritage and values (Kuh, 1985) *and* the advantages of synergy described by Young in Chapter 5. Leadership can be exerted by the president, academic dean, an influential faculty member, or—just as easily and appropriately—the CSAO. There are risks to be sure in taking such bold steps. But the need for leadership has never been greater, and the match of the skills of an effective CSAO to the tasks is excellent.

Second, the meta goal of student affairs, development of the "whole person," is consistent with the goals of general or liberal education (Kuh, Shedd, & Whitt, 1986). On campuses that subscribe to the liberal education tradition, the development of non-intellective qualities including autonomy, emotional stability, and maturity is compatible with knowledge mastery and development of the intellect including critical thinking. On campuses where liberal education—defined as development of the "whole person"—is the preordinate academic mission, faculty embrace teaching and learning and celebrate the connections between cultural and religious heritage, arts and sciences, and intellectual and socio-emotional development. In such settings, the goals of student affairs are compatible with curricular objectives, and student affairs staff can more easily understand and appreciate faculty contributions to students' development.

In this interpretation, the goals of small college faculty and student affairs staff are comparable to a degree rarely approximated on large multi-purpose university campuses where, in general, the liberal education tradition has not fared well. Instead, the holy triumvirate of the academy—Reason, Fact, and Theory—have prevailed almost to the exclusion of other ways of knowing, including the aesthetic (Conrad & Wyer, 1980). In large, research-oriented universities, the importance of knowledge production and specialization within disciplines often overshadows the attention paid to an integrative baccalaureate curriculum. The Germanic tradition of knowledge superiority fostered during graduate school preparation of faculty (and some student affairs staff!) is perpetuated on campuses that consider graduate education as an important mission (Conrad & Wyer, 1980). To take advantage of the similitude between general education and student affairs goals, student affairs staff must first understand and appreciate the supportive, complementary, liberating culture small college faculty endorse before seeking ways to join with the faculty in encouraging students' development.

As a conduit or liaison between the informal and the formal curriculum, the student affairs staff member can help clarify the interconnections between the curriculum and out-of-class experiences for students. Students become cognizant of how accumulating credits and courses is related to the emerging complex plan of choices, values, career and lifelong commitments in relationships, politics, and world concerns. They begin the necessary process of seeing themselves in relationship to the world. The student affairs staff member working within the context of the whole institution functions as a resource in sorting through the puzzle and fitting the pieces together (R. Rood, personal communication, July 23, 1985).

Third, the small college environment is an almost ideal laboratory for encouraging students' active involvement in all forms of learning. The great advantage for both students and student affairs staff is that opportunities for involvement and reinforcement for being involved do not have to be contrived on the small campus. As Hawley and Kuh (Chapter 2) and Young (Chapter 5) pointed out, anonymity is impossible to maintain, and the opportunity subsystem almost demands participation from most students. For student government, athletics, union programming or residence halls to thrive on the small campus, a sizable proportion of the students must be involved. Integration in the academic and social systems of the campus is associated with students' satisfaction, achievement, and persistence (Pascarella, 1980). Involvement—and finding ways to encourage students' *active* involvement in the life of the campus—is the key to fostering students' development (Astin, 1984; Kuh, 1981).

In turn, opportunities for involvement create an environment conducive to leadership development. As Mabey (Chapter 4) noted, the small college is an ideal environment for the intentional development of leadership capabilities. The entire campus can contribute expertise and resources to the mission of fostering leadership development. Preparing students to actively contribute to society has long been a goal of small colleges. The small college learning laboratory provides a context in which the "whole person" can be challenged and enriched.

Taken together, these three factors—a leadership vacuum, the degree of congruence between liberal education and student affairs goals, and the opportunity for active participation of students in the life of the college—suggest that student affairs staff play a critical role on the small college campus. Equally important, the future of student affairs work on the small college looks promising provided student affairs staff and other institutional agents take advantage of these conditions.

A Modest Agenda

There are several things student affairs staff can do to take advantage of the unique conditions indigenous to many small colleges that encourage students' development.

Discover and integrate student affairs into the "organizational saga." Many small colleges have a rich heritage, sometimes connected to a founding religious denomination (Palm, 1984). All institutions have an ethos influenced by this heritage or set of traditions that have evolved over time to comprise a "saga" or story that influences behavior and understandings in the environment (Clark, 1972). The proximity of faculty and staff homes to student residences and campus offices, and the central mission of a liberal arts college—development of the "whole" person—means that the specific functions for which student affairs staff are responsible (e.g., financial aids or career planning and placement) must be interpreted within the ethos of the college.

Student affairs staff would do well to learn and understand as much as possible about the institution's history and its constituent groups. What is important in the institution can only be appreciated by understanding the institution's history and traditions within the current context. Student affairs staff should do everything possible to make certain student development goals and activities of the division are consistent with the mission and saga of the institution (Kuh, 1985), *and* attempt to link some of these traditions to the student affairs mission. For example, the annual performance of Handel's *Messiah* in which two-thirds of the student body participate provides an opportunity for student affairs staff to encourage and reward involvement of residence hall groups, fraternity and sorority members, and others in a living campus tradition. Musically inclined staff can audition for featured parts; less talented staff can join the volunteer chorus. Active support of and involvement in ceremonies that celebrate the institution's heritage, reassert the institution's mission, and perpetuate the institution's "saga" more tightly weave student affairs staff into the social and cultural fabric of the academic community.

Ground policy and action in moral authority. Any educational advantage for small college students, faculty, and student affairs staff springs from a salient institutional purpose. If the small college experience is to instill a shared vision of the future in graduates, the core of values that supports and sustains members of the college community must be consistently communicated to students at every opportunity. For decades, many IHEs, particularly large public universities, have exhibited an uneasy neutrality concerning the role of values in articulating policy and mission, a neutrality that intimates the relative unimportance of values to the educational process (Bok, 1982; Bowen, 1982). This position is unfortunate because, as Bowen (1982) suggested, answers to visionary questions cannot be value-free. "What kind of people do we want our children and grandchildren to be? What kind of society do we want them to live in? How may higher education be guided and shaped to help mature people of this kind create this kind of society?" (p. 9).

The "special vocation" of student affairs staff is to invoke moral authority, grounded in the institution's purpose and heritage, when establishing, interpreting, and applying student life policies (Brown, 1983). The college's core values coupled with philosophical tenets of student affairs work are the touchstones for responsible, value-driven student life programs and practices. Without moral authority, the vision of the college and the goals of the student affairs unit become blurred. Without moral authority, passion and principle are empty.

The quality of society is partly a function of the degree to which fundamental questions—such as those proposed by Bowen—are considered by students during college. The small college has been and must continue to be a building block of an enlightened society. Student affairs staff are uniquely positioned to enhance the potent influence of college attendance on students' values.

Participate in as many dimensions of campus life as possible. One way to do this is to play different roles in the college community as appropriate. For example, a chapel or convocation address has ceremonial value in that faculty, students, and student affairs colleagues will perceive student affairs as an integral part of the community. The experience also will enrich the staff member's perspective if additional layers of meaning are attached to the importance of convocation to the campus culture. Similarly, attendance at and participation in the faculty senate (or facsimile) provides first hand information about the concerns and issues considered important by faculty.

Come to "know" students and "know" faculty. On the surface, this seems to be so obvious that it is almost offensive. But a combination of psycho-social personal development issues specific to many student affairs staff, an increasingly heterogeneous student body, and beliefs in and reliance on positivism and "analytical science" (i.e., the pervasive belief in Western culture that "science" provides "certainty" through precision, accuracy, and reliability) interact to threaten the assumptions we use to "know" and understand persons in our environment (Mitroff & Kilmann, 1978).

Entry level and some mid-level student affairs staff between the ages of 23 and 33 typically encounter personal development issues related to status and identity within the field of student affairs work and security in the institutional setting. We advise student affairs colleagues (a) to resist the tendency to act as if they have the "answers" or "solutions" to all problems, (b) to be more willing to admit uncertainty, and (c) to actively pursue collaboration with those faculty and students who exhibit a willingness in learning more about campus problems and concerns. Stereotypes about faculty often break down through collaborative activities pursued in a collegial spirit. The better we get to know our faculty colleagues, the more similarities we may discover between "them" and us. Pretty soon, like Pogo, we discover "them" has been "us" all along.

Most small college faculty are readily accessible and spend a considerable amount of time with students. Therefore, compared with their university counterparts the perceived need for small college student affairs staff to be considered "expert" about student development or student attitudes may not be as great. While student development theory is helpful in anticipating certain kinds of behaviors, a little knowledge can be dangerous if misused. For example, if one expects first-year students to lack confidence and be unable to adequately manage emotions, one will surely look for and find behaviors that confirm these hypotheses. We must come to know students, faculty, and ourselves as persons and be reluctant to rely—without healthy skepticism—on theory, research, and mythology when attempting to understand human behavior.

Advocate for students but only when consistent with the mission of the college. Championing students' rights and causes is a noble purpose. While we are responsible for understanding students and current issues pertaining to the student life mission of the college, we cannot always support a position taken by students (if there is only one position!); at times, student affairs staff must articulate the institution's principles and remain steadfast when pressures are brought by students that could compromise the integrity of the student affairs division and what the college stands for. The student voice must be recognized as legitimate; but blind advocacy is not as important as respect and inclusion behavior, based on moral authority, from institutional agents and peers.

To the extent possible, blur distinctions between student affairs staff, faculty, and academic administrators. Compared with the multi-university, institutional agents are more likely to share the same preordinate goal in a small college with a distinctive liberal arts mission—education of the "whole person." A salient mission often coupled with cultural and religious traditions serves as a bellwether and gives direction to faculty, students, and staff. Relatively little ambiguity exists in the small college environment about what is appropriate and inappropriate behavior.

Students' development is not the exclusive domain of the "student development" office or student affairs staff. Indeed, student development (intellectual, affective, psycho-motor) *is* the *raison d'être* of the college. Therefore, student affairs staff are advised to *teach* something. Faculty rank is not as important as making, and being *perceived by faculty* as making, valued contributions to the primary mission of the institution.

Another way of blurring the distinctions between student affairs staff and faculty is to avoid using language from the student affairs "rain forest" (Kuh, 1985; Schroeder, Nicholls & Kuh, 1983). Buzz words and jargon can be useful but only within the "tribe" (i.e., student affairs staff). It is incumbent that faculty be educated about the role and complementarity of the student affairs mission with the institution's purpose. However, the language used to describe student affairs contributions to the college must be from general education treatises (e.g., Boyer & Kaplan, 1977), not from textbooks written for graduate students or from a Myers-Briggs typology workshop. This is not to demean knowledge generated specifically to increase efficacious behavior in the field. Rather, student affairs staff must remain cognizant that for such information to be understandable and useful to others, it must be translated into terms that have meaning for all groups on the campus.

Monitor and record students' involvement in the life of the college. The wave of educational reform reports has spilled over into postsecondary education, and assessing students' progress during college has become an important agenda item (Ewell, 1985). Student affairs staff are uniquely positioned to monitor the extent to which students actively participate in various aspects of the college experience (Astin, 1985). Merely being "close" to students is not enough. We must take seriously our responsibility for encouraging and documenting students' involvement in social and academic activities.

Crookston (1976) envisioned a learning environment in which students, educators, and social systems interact and encourage students' personal growth through responding to developmental tasks. Bowen (1977) and Mable (1980) recommended personal growth assessments so that students can monitor their own progress on various developmental dimensions. Student growth plans or portfolios are one way to record students' progress during college. Monitoring and recording should begin during orientation and continue through graduation. Brown and DeCoster (1982) provide some illustrative checklists that student affairs staff can consult when encouraging students to develop a personal growth plan.

As interest in assessment gains momentum within institutions and professional associations, questions about documenting student gains during college will become more sophisticated. Attention is now focused on how much one learns during college, but more subtle measures reflecting changes in cognitive or intellectual development may become important (Kuh, 1981). Student affairs staff with experience in developing and scoring instruments designed to assess intellectual development can make important contributions to the institutional research program. Equally important, information about students' participation in musical groups, student government, intramurals, and other activities will be invaluable to the college's enrollment management strategy as prospective students will expect to find indices of student participation in campus life reported in promotional material (Kuh & Wallman, 1986).

Collecting and interpreting this information in concert with campus design data (Chapter 2) will provide an occasion to reaffirm whether what is happening to students is desirable, and if not, what should be done to change the situation. This is a complex process often confounded by emphasizing efficiency (i.e., how well student affairs staff are performing) rather than efficacy (i.e., why we do what we do and what we hope to accomplish) (Bowen, 1974). By recording what students do with their time, student affairs staff and students will have an informed perspective from which to determine if they are doing the right things, rather than doing things right.

Conclusion

Student affairs staff can make important contributions to the culture and sense of community of a small college. Our worth is related to the extent to which: (a) we perform well the multiple roles we have accepted, (b) we are intimately acquainted with and involved in diverse aspects of institutional life; (c) we collaborate with and encourage collaboration among faculty, students, and colleagues, and (d) we nurture and respect the importance of developing deep, meaningful relationships—with students and others.

Student affairs roles and goals complement the central mission of the academy and support as well as embellish contributions of faculty and others in the academic community. Our success is shared with faculty and students and is measured by the extent to which the small college becomes, for most students, a developmentally powerful experience, and alumni reflect the distinctive character and culture of the institution. The tasks are many, the challenges profound, and the legacy important to the well-being not only of the small college but of society as well.

References

Astin, A. W. (1977). *Four critical years.* San Francisco, CA: Jossey-Bass.

Astin, A. W. (1984). Student involvement: A developmental theory for higher education. *Journal of College Student Personnel, 25,* 297- 308.

Astin, A. W. (1985). Involvement: The cornerstone of excellence. *Change, 17* (4), 35-39.

Bok, D. (1982). *Beyond the ivory tower.* Cambridge, Mass.: Harvard University Press.

Bowen, H. R. (1974) (Ed.). Evaluating institutions for accountability. *New Directions for Institutional Research,* No. 1. San Francisco: Jossey-Bass.

Bowen, H. R. (1977). *Investment in learning.* San Francisco: Jossey- Bass.

Bowen, H. R. (1982). *The state of the nation and the agenda for higher education.* San Francisco: Jossey-Bass.

Boyer, E. L., & Kaplan, M. (1977). *Educating for survival.* New Rochelle, NY: Change Magazine Press.

Brown, R. D. (1983). Editorial: A common vision. *Journal of College Student Personnel. 24,* 3-5.

Brown, R. D., & DeCoster, D. A. (Eds.) (1982). Mentoring-transcript systems for promoting student growth. *New Directions for Student Services,* No. 19. San Francisco: Jossey-Bass.

Carnegie Foundation for the Advancement of Teaching (1985). The liberal arts perspective. *Change, 17* (4), 31-33.

Clark, B. R. (1972). The organizational saga in higher education. *Administrative Science Quarterly, 17,* 178-184.

Conrad, C. F., & Wyer, J. C. (1980). *Liberal education in transition.* AAHE-ERIC/ Higher Education Research Report No. 3. Washington, D.C.: American Association for Higher Education.

Crookston, B. B. (1976). Education for human development. In C. F. Warmath (Ed.). *New Directions for College Counselors.* San Francisco: Jossey-Bass.

Ewell, P. (1985). Assessment: What's it all about. *Change, 17* (6), 32-36.
Hossler, D. (1984). *Enrollment management: An integrated approach.* Princeton, N.J.: College Board.
Kuh, G. D. (1981). *Indices of quality in the undergraduate experience.* AAHE-ERIC/ Higher Education Research Report No. 4. Washington, D.C.: American Association for Higher Education.
Kuh, G. D. (1985). What is extraordinary about ordinary student affairs organizations. *NASPA Journal, 23* (2), 31-43
Kuh, G. D., Shedd, J., & Whitt, E. (April, 1986). *Student affairs and liberal education: Unrecognized common law partners.* Paper presented to the meeting of the American College Personnel Association, New Orleans.
Kuh, G. D., & Wallman, G. H. (1986). Outcomes oriented marketing. In D. Hossler (Ed.), Managing collegiate enrollments. *New Directions for Higher Education.* San Francisco: Jossey-Bass.
Mable, P. (1980). Student development perspectives and strategies in the assessment of student needs. In D. Creamer (Ed.). *Student development in higher education* (pp. 229-238). Cincinnati, OH: American College Personnel Association.
Mitroff, I. I., & Kilmann, R. H. (1978). *Methodological approaches to social science.* San Francisco: Jossey-Bass.
Pace, C. R. (1982). *Achievement and quality of student effort.* Los Angeles, CA: Higher Education Research Institute, University of California.
Palm, R. L. (1984). Student personnel administration at the small college. *NASPA Journal, 22* (2), 48-54.
Pascarella, E. T. (1980). Student-faculty informal contact and college outcomes. *Review of Educational Research, 50,* 545-595.
Reich, R. B. (1983). *The next American frontier: A provocative program for economic renewal.* New York: Time Books.
Schroeder, C. C., Nicholls, G. E., & Kuh, G. D. (1983). Exploring the rain forest: Testing assumptions and taking risks. In G. Kuh (Ed.), Understanding student affairs organizations, *New Directions for Student Services, No. 23,* (pp. 51-65). San Francisco: Jossey-Bass.
Study Group on the Conditions of Excellence in American Higher Education (1984). *Involvement in learning: Realizing the potential of American higher education.* Washington, D. C.: National Institute of Education.